Limberlost II
The Legacy

Spiderwize
Remus House
Coltsfoot Drive
Woodston
Peterborough
PE2 9BF

www.spiderwize.com

At last; the rest of the story…

LIMBERLOST II

The Legacy

An epilogue to Limberlost

by

RICKY DALE

LIMBERLOST II; The Legacy

Set along the ambling south shore of Lake Ontario, the summers are lazy and the winters mostly sympathetic. It is here that the narrative begins and shifts to and fro between the infant years of the 20th century and to more latterly times.

Limberlost II; The Legacy is an aesthetically beguiling story about an heterogeneous 'family' who all share a similar comparability. This emotionally poignant explanation is of the secret and the sin that bonds them. It is a semi-fictional tears and delight account of their unknowing path to redemption.

By the very essence of its personal nature their story is a sufficiently complex yet simple way, how the tensions and alterations of inner and outer experiences can affect every one of us.

The result is one of the most realistic and exceptional semi-fictional pictures of, not necessarily ones self plus society's self, but of ones self without society.

It is for certain that the honesty and the sheer punchiness of each unpretentious protagonist will continue to be a part of your psyche; long after you've reluctantly finished reading the final paragraph of this novel.

ACKNOWLEDGEMENTS AND SPECIAL THANKS

In addition to my publisher and to the sources listed on the copyright page of this book; I also owe much to the following good folk, whose interest in my writing I consider to be the highest possible complement ever achieved.

First and foremost my daughter, Dr KIMBERLEY JAYNE, for all her invaluable support, in addition to the tolerance of enduring my idiosyncratic prose versus her academicism! And to TRISH ASHLEY, whose praiseworthy observations carried me along. To Montrealler DIANNE LETKY, who for years patiently assessed each chapter I forwarded to her and who never lost faith. A very grateful thank you also to KAYE BRZOZKA for her most diligent proof reading, typing and appraisal. Thanks to PAT RISELY; from the outset you've promoted me and been a pillar of encouragement. Much gratitude also to PETE LAYLAND at Action Stationers for years of unfailing reliability. And to JANICE and ROBERT WEBBER who generated the "Legacy" title. Last but not least, my friend TIM SIMS, and my brother "UNCLE" MIKE for your many notions and "bent" ears!

Special thanks besides to ZOE HATHERALL of Black Cat Books, St Marychurch, for always keeping me in-stock. And to all the sweet people of ST MARYCHURCH and ANVILLE whose encouragement has been significant to me; I am indebted to you as well.

Ricky Dale

AUTHOR'S NOTE

Especially for Kim and for Mom & Jacque; and for those of you who kindly asked, and indeed for anyone else with such curiosity; here is the rest of the story for you.

In the event that you have not read LIMBERLOST book I, this second book may not stand by itself for you. However, for those of you who have read the first book, I am sure that you will find, amongst other things, many answers to your questions, and many new surprises.

The LIMBERLOST novels all spring from actual events and fact as I remember it; although how dull life would be, without blending in a smidgen of fiction!

Ricky Dale

****Contents****

****Principal characters****

Kim - Birth name Krystyna - Lyric Soprano

Sandra - Concert Pianist

Mom - Aka Lillian - Restaurateur

Bliss Carmen - Lillian's mother

Jacques Leyrac - Impresario extraordinaire

Dahlia Carrière - Showgirl

Joe Burke - Cowboy

George Zalokostas - Chicken Farmer

Tony Barber - Barber

Bob 'Mitcham' - m'etier unknown

<u>and fleetingly...</u>

Redvers Lamar-Smith - Mayor

Jim Castellano - Organisation member

PROLOGUE

Krystyna was ably mindful of each and every evolving step she had laboriously trodden during her long and arduous journey homeward - on all occasions, always tight-lipped and proud. In her unique exacting fashion always predictably unpredictable - though blithely unaware of it.

Although she had rarely felt genuinely optimistic with regard to achieving her elusive journeys end (or for that matter recognising it in the event of its arrival) nonetheless her inner voice of expectation for 'something' to happen kept pressing her forward. It was uncannily similar to being expropriated by some unimaginable hero-worshipping audience and passively endeavouring to trace an escape path through the speckled star-crossed agony of their fantasisations...when your own eyes and voice have entirely disappeared.

Come what may, now at last she was home and all of the pages of her ongoing story are blank, cleansed and impressionless - at least until the inevitable word, sentence or smudge is unwarily inked upon them

Despite all of those unproductive connotations of hopeless hopefulness and languishment, it is still nevertheless comparatively mystifying to what precisely became of those 'irritable' imprints of yesteryear? Although the 'fever' has been put right, does the uncompromising antidote really cure the awful symptoms? Or have they been more inclined to stretch out and grow more vivid - perhaps sometimes more beautiful - periodically more ugly - predominantly more significant and deeper?

Every so often it is as if her twin soul were travelling a parallel path but in an opposite direction of a shared circle - drifting fancifully free and waiting to be called upon to halt - checking circle after circle for the elusive answer. It was in those quiet moments of perspicacity that she pondered upon the residue of ruefulness that repeatedly seemed to dictate her life. Quite often it became a gamble for her to choose or to ignore an invitation; to make the transition into a further adjustment or not to. There seemed to be multiples of uncertainties that were resilient to any type of reasoning. However on this occasion she felt sure that her assessment was correct - like a performer in front of her first audience she wanted to spectacularly rise to the response.

I sense her looking pensively away from me toward a pause in space. Like the unpredictable colours in an indescribable sunset she is already beginning to understand how to merge and how to separate herself from herself. When anxiously I allow my index finger free rein to write an interpretation of her mood (in whatever safety of certainty that mood may be) I find it quite impossible to second-guess let alone transliterate wholly or even partly its intrinsicness.

I try to manoeuvre my way back into her thinking again and tentatively listen to her speaking; I have the impression that she is not speaking of her own experiences anymore, but of some other person she once knew. It seems that at times she becomes an outsider who is staring through her own window at a party that she has not been invited to just yet. She is indeed Mon Amie La Rose who hasn't so far been able to make its choice between the pasture and the lawn. And even so, as she speaks every word begins to fly so freely and to such a sanguine degree that you hope some insuperable miracle will happen and miraculously alter everything that needs the altering for her.

And when quite suddenly she becomes silent and lost in thought again, even that silence has become impossible to ignore; it chatters incessantly almost as though an eternity of silence was really meant to be the norm.

It seems to me that in this worldly-wise universe that is critically cynical to puritivity and spontaneous chuckles; she has been endowed with the gift to give reason to the abjects that used to permeate her life, and the countless perky possibilities that she has brought back for herself. With this mind-set maybe now, even sadness and darkness can no longer lurk seductively just below the surface - although she has long since grown accustomed to them, and at times she has become thankful for them to return.

CHAPTER I
Krystyna

Krystyna Comanescu was the immaculate master of decor - the quintessential Madonna of art; in her own particular way it was a deep-rooted fulfilment that was totally enjoyable and obsessively inexorable. From her fine-shadow eyes to the rinky-dink spectacles upon her nose, every relatively unimportant facet was conscientiously orchestrated, and owned its own deliberately created place to be!

Unsurprisingly, to produce something to meet a person's individual requirements could not be measured in proverbial hours and minutes; and for that reason it was necessary for her to nurture and reward her painstaking pertinacity with a playtime pleasure.

At whatever time the sun was singing in her head and on whatever occasion the distinctive aroma of fresh percolating coffee pervaded the air; and the chock-full pails were splashed to brimming with tasty new blanched potatoes - and stiffened tablecloths arrayed the burnished expectant cutlery and fine-sprinkling cruets. Only at a time such as this when every eventuality of an inrush is prepared with such pristine readiness; only then with all these things considered could Krystyna reward her self-induced productiveness with her own special self-congratulatory indulgence. Fleet-footed she could, now melt away and luxuriate in carte blanch interims of intimacy alongside the sloping evergreens on the grassy banks of Winter Creek.

It was not at all as though Krystyna's self-indulgent predispositions were likely to impose any type of selfish (or rash) impediment upon her business. To the contrary it was without doubt that Anville folks heartily endorsed her somewhat moxie resourcefulness...as a mere 'gal' restaurateur!

Indeed in most minds her 'semi-reclusive' skedaddling routine was surely damn all any persons' obligation to opinionise about. And anyways there was not ever an occasion when her whereabouts would not respond to a 'yell' - and that was the all important resolve, and nothing more besides!

Tactfully speaking it could be argued that traditionally the tendency of some local country folk was to regard 'showbizzy' types with a certain tendency of single mindedness in any event. It was pretty-much assumed that the conduct of such 'troupers' would no doubt tend to be imprudent and zany at the very least!

However, most folk seemed to be made up of good intentions and that was all Krystyna desired. In fact she never really found that anyone's 'evaluations' were problematic to her. She had been endowed with her own explanation of the unintelligible past and the unambiguous present - they were

5

her ownership, for better or for worse. She did not feel obliged to justify them. From time to time the unpleasant recollections would sneak slyly by, but Krystyna was able to get up above them, sanitize them and make even the most crabby thoughts into positive thoughts.

All through the long-lasting summer days - with the rebirth of green grass and the threaded circlets of daisies leaving their fine powder in her hair. And those many sticky handfuls of wilting dandelions arranged fondly in a medley of canisters like Netherlands tulips. And Krystyna somewhat unbecoming in Bermudan shorts cradling her callow face at knee length - pensively watching the snappy turtles, watchfully sloe-eyeing her sad expression in return.

All throughout the plentiful short-winded summer nights - hot flushed and bored by feverish bed linen; far better being the surreptitious mistress to the grazing corn-fed moon; resting furtively beneath the cornflower sky. Rising from her bed like an indolent butterfly and dizzy dancing in the fresh midnight air; cavorting with the trees, dazzling the myriad lights of gazillions of stars; playing hide-and-seek with her half forgotten self-awareness, this had evermore been her dream - now at last it was her reality.

All the way through those curt winter days and the much too dead, self-expansive winter nights; when misconceptions can become reality and sometimes reality can become indifferent. Like a mute swan restlessly rousing itself into wakefulness -

silent, rested and peeking cautiously through the colourless half-light of dawn. She would slip swiftly into her gladiolus psychedelic most brawny winter coat and blinking slightly blurred, step out into the sobering north bound wind. Her nursling fruit trees wailing for shelter – the grey-blue underbushes grasping at the hemming of her over exposed nightclothes. Krystyna so unfazed; like a somewhat concerted master baker with a determined schedule to follow - she laboriously begins her spread and scatter routine. Extravagant rich full-handed cobs of golden maize with lovingly baked broken communion wholewheat - for the tiny claws and jaws of all possible fauna's woebegone companions.

Her life and the loves in her life have been blissfully unfurled - the inconsolable is no longer credible; it is as though it had progressed all it dared and now its swarthy stain had been erased for evermore.

CHAPTER II

Sandra

Sandra was more than happy about her elasticated illusion of reality. In any event she had never valued reality itself as being interestingly that important. With innumerable bravura sequences of frenzied artistry beneath her girdle; why indeed would she find it necessary to stoop and value the fetish of semi-authenticity for even an instant?

The familiarity of fame and ostentation had italicized this extraordinary and somewhat legendary ladybug from out of her cane break provenance. Like it tends to capture most dexterous artiste's; and that was every bit the gist of it!

The immortalized magical land of skyscrapers and concert halls; of the Metropolitan; Carnegie Hall; Broadway, Fifth Avenue and Washington Square, And feeling cross-eyed at the presence of Brooklyn Bridge beneath your feet, and the seemingly intuitive understanding of being a home-girl who has come home, from the very first instant of enplaning at Kennedy.

From time to time when cranky society feels it necessary to frustrate a person's intimate desires and instincts (sometimes to the unfortunate extent that they can never really be clearly identified again) Sandra could become quite riled. She was the most accomplished adversary to that type of unwarranted

8

adversity. It was as though she was a 'rum pot' who became intoxicated by the sheer audacity of humankind and its persnicketyness; it was like a clowns overdose to her. Sandra would walk upon the very air that they breathed, barefoot if necessary! If they dared to pique her sense of humour (and some of her erstwhile critics would try) she would look toward them with such a mighty numbus 'tour de force' that it felt as though God was reading their pulse. In the event that all else failed, she would meticulously push her chair back and walk with a dignified tread from the room. Indeed Jacques Leyrac had donned her the phrase "demonstrate your experience" and she had memorised his advice precisely.

CHAPTER III

Mom

July just seemed to arrive unpardonably out of the blue, in a sudden attack of blistering, burning heat; breathlessly transcending South Western Ontario's heartland into the finest orchard garden glasshouse in the world. And at the savouring conclusion of every day, when all the fields and forests are luxuriant and suntanned and the potent earth is becoming warm again: a sticky oloroso permeates the air and sympathetically moisturises the hurrying whisper of twilight.

By the second, by the minute, by the hour, each Limberlost peach tree begins to synchronously unburden their day's industry. Each and every peach full and fat, succulent and ripe, wavering and falling to earth: a first, a second, a third, a pair, and long before the sweat of sunup approaches again, multitudes!

There were so, so many roly-poly clientele from out of town who couldn't and really didn't care less with regard to the gratuitous collecting of calories. Therefore this auspicious occasion became their avail to 'pig-out' on moms rich and outrageously scrumptious 'peach' desserts: by and large (the emphasis on 'Large') they comprised of: peach short torte, peach mouse and peach shortcake, splendid supplementarys to grace any restaurateurs' bill of fare! However after dismissing the gourmandised out-of-towners, the U.S. Tourists and such folk, it was categorically the most serious misdemeanour and woe betide to ever even contemplate offering those miserable 'cast-off' fruits to any of Moms 'illustrious' local denizens. In this respect Mom was ever so watchful of her dippy waitresses.

Mom had always succeeded in keeping matters under control, despite the occasional difficulty; she was a survivor and knew how to muddle through; at least that was the positivity she portrayed. She seemed to have this ability to identify a person at first contact and to know them through and through; almost as though she had come across them sometime, somewhere before. All the more, she could even predict a person's mood, their feelings and to some extent, their inclinations; to a far greater degree than any so-called clairvoyant could. It was quite strange to observe; once she had reckoned on the score, she would simply sit back and hang loose; it was as though she had made her assessment and now she could relax and watch the drama unfold! Perhaps Moms secret was that she was an incredibly universal lady, who knew that you had to be local to be universal.

Now, having said all that, it was Moms peculiar dexterity (and exceptional diversity) that seemed to have beset her with uneasiness, and that from time to time could make her private life difficult to endure (or at least give reason to).

In the latterly period of her autumn years (especially in her evenings of calm) disquiet would prey upon her peace of mind and ruffle her usual self-assurance. It would invariably ask her the same unanswerable question: of whether (or not) she could be capable or ever likely of finding an ideally suited person to snug down with. Whether (or not) fidelity and compatibility could be hers, during the front porch summers and the snowbound winters. She oftentimes would say a 'rough and tumble' type of prayer but despite her satire she desperately wanted (nay needed) the extravagance of besottedness to happen, to be real, and to be present and alive. She really desired to discover one lovely stupid day when at last she was able to grasp the gift and unthinkingly throw her life's caution to the wind. To be offered such was beyond her wildest imagination and comprehension but not ever beyond her unceasing hopefulness and her innumerable dreams.

"GONE WERE BUT THE WINTER COME WERE BUT THE SPRING"

Christina Rossetti

At around sunset on Saturday August 18th, 1968, under the most vast patient skies, Mom roped and put her brand on one of North America's enduring legends: the 'cowboy'. After an entire life time of being exceptionally circumspect, cautious, wary and carefully selective, she was full-blown 90 degrees in Love!

Sufficient to add that at least the situation was not compounded by sex, and therefore it was not too difficult to negotiate; well that was what they had us believe!

In any event it was all quite simple. Mom had offered him some advice regarding getting married, and he had accepted it!

All in all it had turned out to be a great wedding day, a family day, a universal day for a universal lady; a day in which even Mom became a little disorientated. She was unaccustomed to as much care and attention, and adored it!

"COWBOYS AREN'T DEAD. YOU JUST CANT SEE THEM FROM THE HIGHWAY"

a 'wrangler'

It had all begun at Anville's annual rodeo when the populace would swell to capacity. It was a main event and a gathering that would draw Stetson hats and dust-smudged faces from Texas, Oklahoma and north from Colorado: the most skilful, the damp greenhorns and the drink excessively entrants who can hardly crawl to their motel rooms! Nevertheless they were all heroes for their few seconds in mid air; and then the mud and the dust; but hats retrieved, Levi's dusted and it's back to the bull pen again!

For the most part Anville village folk grew up with the myth of the cowboy on the movie and TV screen, rather than (in general terms) the reality of hardship and endless enduring on the flipside of the myth. The core reality was of inexorable change, of the Wal-Mart sprawl, of interstates ploughing up the plains and the unique big endless skies being carved up by ungainly pylons. However during the latter half of August (living for several weeks or less) romantic notions of life on the range were unambiguously permitted. For the time being the eternal non-

13

parallel between "invention" and "actuality" could leastways be forgotten. At this precise moment in time Mom is Joan Crawford's audacious 'Vienna' – the strong-willed business women in the wilderness of Arizona, and Joe Burke (her beau from Bow River) is her one-shot lover Sterling Hayden - the very reticent 'Johnny Guitar'.

Having explained all that, perhaps there 'is' a parallel between "invention and actuality" after all; or at least the possibility of such. Perhaps this similarity is found in the homogeneously red penned words inscribed on notepaper sellotaped to Moms restaurant entrance door:-

"LEAVE YOUR GUNS AT THE DOOR BOYS"

Followed by the literal enticement:—

"FREE COFFEE AND FRIES"

It all worked out, and it was a good day when he left his gun at her door. He knew his bones had become too brittle to ride bulls and she knew what a journeyman's glance meant. Perhaps though, no more Omaha, Dallas or San Antonio in the fall, their Cheyenne autumn has tied them with golden thread, leastways until ten minutes, ten hours or ten years; it's all the same when you don't have to say goodbye.

CHAPTER IV

The Man with the Red Pontiac Bonneville

It's sort of worried some folk because ever since Mom had up sticks and moved on, odd things seemed to have been happening in Anville for some time: Lilacs bloom in January; children fall in love before birth and Zeb the fossiled face truck driver has become a poet and opened a vegetarian diner, which incidentally sells plum brandy in pint glasses! And who, for God's goodness sake is the secretive man with the red Pontiac Bonneville; who fairly looks like Robert Mitcham and whose kid is covered with bug-bites?

Out on RR1# Highway 21, Anville was like an alleyway that had cut through time and paused. Although it had always preserved its fabled simplistic tradition, from time to time there was nevertheless a postponed sob for the outside world; particularly from the progressive younger generation. As for the muzzy, venerable oldsters; well for the most part they were becoming almost as fabled as the village itself! They were definitely more inclined to glide through their recollections in warm slippers and rose-coloured spectacles. The Godforsaken suggestion that somewhere in so called recent history the Inca Empire may have collapsed was to be totally ignored for its absurdity. However it was impossible to ignore that the intervention of Bell telephone was nothardly such a bad thing; or so they say!

But it was a fact that the lay of the land was unquestionable changing; as sure as eggs is eggs. Even now at this very moment, its furthermost boundaries are widening and it no longer seems possible for the village to remain an isolate indefinitely. Even the most chipper folk were beginning to second guess that their world within a world was no longer the way that they perceived it to be. The spotless attire of 20th Century hermits was becoming tarnished and eccentric by the windstorm of progress.

Take Tony's one-chair barbershop for instance. Men still come for a cut, a splash and a little news but business is getting slower. Tony says "younger guys go to those, you know, hairdressers". It seems like most of his business these days consists of old fellows and guys he went to school with. Maybe even a few of his grandfather's customers and he's been gone 55 years!

Tony had stopped wearing the traditional white smock barbers uniform several years ago. It's mostly jeans, t-shirt and slippers now and a "Ring Bell for Service" sign just inside the shop door.

There was a time when it was good to look up at the sky during a bright summer's day and to know that the night stars are still there above your head; even though you can't actually see them, it's kind of reassuring to know that they are still shining brightly for you. But now and then, just lately, there are one or two negative stars that endeavour to darken and freeze the landscape with indifference and confusion.

Perhaps the elusive answer is found in the palms of the stars —
perhaps the order of things has already been predetermined; or
could it be that contrary to pessimistic suggestion the better part
of the community have not been blinded by the enriching rays of
many bright stars - could it be that now is the time to stare back
at those negative black rays until defeated, they whiten!

CHAPTER V

Red Stick Louisiana

Over at the 'new' coffee house an old man in a sun bleached suit and maple leaf hat, sat hunched at the end of the counter and sipped his coffee from a spoon. A sassy mannered waitress of somewhat ample proportions bounced across the floppy floorboards toward him. "Here you are Mr Zalokostas, the best pumpkin pie in Anville".

"I'm obliged" he replied in a quiet voice. George stirred sugar into his coffee and sampled the pie, it was delicious!

He glanced over the top of his spectacles at the potpourri bowls and pizzazz decor; too clinical, more like a 'dunny' he thought. "Lived here long" said the waitress in a probing voice. George looked up, he normally liked big ladies but she was somehow irritatingly yappy; and he didn't like that. Clearing her throat as she spoke, she iterated "strange name Anville, it's the oddest name for a town that I've ever heard of; what the goddamned does it supposed to mean "she added sarcastically".

George hardly had the energy to reply but he felt he must. He had a sense of high-mindedness about his town, it had given him his bread and butter for years and she was just disrespecting – her Johnny cake isn't done in the middle or something he thought. "There's plenty towns that have funny names", he said.

18

What of Saskatoon and Whistler, what is the meaning of them then?

He straightened up and looked at her, his elderly eyes blue and furious. "When we were fighting the war my companion was a private from Baton Rouge, Louisiana; now there's a helluva name for a town, Red Stick, Louisiana, what d'ya think of that?

She glared several daggers at the thin white-haired native; "Don't forget your umbrella and hat when you leave" and buttoning up her overall to the neck she began to noisily refill the condiments.

George stared passively into his empty coffee cup, it had taken all his wind to reply to her; perhaps he had been a little harsh but in any event he would not be welcome here again, that was for sure!

He could sense her seething as he made his way to the entrance door, "growing pains" he thought, "she just has growing pains".

It would take too long to explain to her that Anville is not merely a static name; it is an entity, it has its own distinctive existence: it changes and fluctuates; sometimes weaker, sometimes stronger, depending on how you want or need it to be, that's how it becomes.

His blue eyes foggy, he surmised "Right now I feel that my town is disappearing altogether, - and me with it".

CHAPTER VI
Symphony No. 5

The snow arrived early in '82 which was usually the case after an unnecessary Indian summer. By Remembrance Day (Nov 11th) the sombre meadows were beginning to be slowly and silently blotted out. And before the first week of December, Anville's Main Street was lined on either side by peaked mountains of snow; periodically pushed there by the town sharp-nosed plough.

Limberlost lay hushed and still, but for all that Kim was taking the lack of trade quite philosophically and was sat at the counter chewing absentmindedly on a ring-shaped donut, desultorily listening to Mahler's Adagietto No. 5 parodying the snowflakes!

Kim adored the tranquillity of mornings like these— singularly unusual mornings when it seemed that the whole world had returned itself to itself, when pulchritude was the only essential necessary. Her sentiments were somewhat self-indulgent, but they were hers and hers alone and that was all that really mattered. Was it only several weeks ago that she had taken down the rolled protective sun awning from the restaurant windows? "t'will nevermore be May again" she thought whimsically. Here in her place of honour at the top of the table of life, it almost seemed that she was able to make those sentiments come true!

CHAPTER VII

The "Banquet Room" & Tony. George. Bob

'Banquet Room' must have seemed a ridiculously ostentatious nameplate to ever attach to such a nondescript, non-essential storeroom at the backend of a restaurant. The provenance for a name of such a high degree must have been masterminded by an individual with a God-powerful imagination. Or there again perhaps it was a deliberate exaggeration of the truth: a hyperbolic subterfuge to boastfully advise the outside world of the regular occurrence of banquets in boondock Anville? Or maybe it was none of the aforementioned reasons whatsoever; or maybe it was all of them and others? However, partially if not entirely the answer for such eloquently grandiose parentage lies indubitably in the somewhat distant past, conceivably around the period when the notoriety of the name "Limberlost" begun.

As far back as we need to go is close to or approaching the 1890's. It was during this portion of time that Bliss and Earle Carmen purchased a small amount of prime acreage, just south of Winter Creek, from a shrewd land agent named Tom Swain. Tom was in the "Lost and found" business of a sort, he would procure surrendered Indian land from the government and sell it off for a tidy profit. It was initially the Carmen's intention to farm crops and herbs and to provide food and lodging for paying guests. However after only several years into the venture Earle unexpectedly died of pneumonia, during the winter of '99, leaving

Bliss and their youngster pretty much destitute.

Tom Swain had always been rather sweet on Bliss, and for a while he helped her to finish off the building construction work – that was until his wife began assuming about Toms obsession, and that was the end of that!

Bliss was not one iota fatalistic about the future; she had never lent herself to so-called normative reasoning. Whilst Mrs Conventional wouldn't consider it prudent to stretch their feet longer than their blankets, Bliss was not a person who believed in accepting her 'Lot' and making-do with what she had on offer. And it was this inventive resourcefulness and her canny knowledge of "home economics" that imbued her with a quality of folk legend status. Whilst it was her sweet bread and flaky pie crusts that brought her notability, obversely it was her impressive knowledge of spirituous liquors that brought her notoriety! Bliss was kind of fond of keeping secrets and would not avail herself to allow any person, not anyone to be acquainted with the ingredients of her potent potion; in accordance with that maxim the basement remained continuously locked, particularly when she was in 'production'. If asked regarding the constituents of the concoction she would invariably reply: "Strychnine, the curse of God and old rye", it'll make you babble to owls and galoshes; you had better believe it!

Bliss knew one hundred percent exactly what the town wanted and she provided it; abundantly!

22

During the length of time it had taken to repeal the Volstead act, Bliss had become the grande dame of franchising to half the population of Anville. The other half felt more inclined to just drink it!

Another attribute chalked-up to Bliss was her interchangeable disposition; at least on a local level. Her renowned "Mommies Libation" instigated her election as chairman of the Temperance Society; and a founding member of the Anti-Saloon League, well it seems that women were welcomed to speakeasies and largely barred from saloons in any event.

Perhaps it had never entered the minds of the noble-ladies of abstemiousness that "Mommies Libation" was purely an impure oxymoron, and to a degree so was Bliss Carmen!

"Said the voice of Evil to the ear of Good"
"Clasp thou my strong right hand, nor shall our clasp be known
or understood by any in the Land"
Isabella Valancy Crawford, "Gisli the Chieftain" 1905

Now this is where the Banquet Room was conceived and came into its own. The dub "Banquet" implied 'major league'; it was a meeting place where friends from the community and 'organised' acquaintances from across the border could rendezvous: in order to discuss the financial advantages of illicitly distilled proscription and such.

In order to provide the room with a more ritzy kind of ambience, Bliss hired a woodworker to timber lath the walls and ceiling with reddish-brown mahogany type wood; and a hydro guy to enhance the walls with intermittent lighting.

There are numerous accounts of illustrious and imprudent rogues and clients who entered the portals of Bliss's judicious establishment: the lawful and the lawless: flappers, judges, cabdrivers and cops. And the nameless faces who had fought, drunk, loved and sadly sometimes had died.

The banknotes bustled and spilled over and across the grassy slopes of the Niagara escarpment during those seemingly illimitable elementary years of our 20th Century.

Well, even God has ever been known to cheat anyone for being keen-eyed and quick witted, not even in the world of greed he created. However, sooner or later every mover and shaker needs to get nearer to the fire, assuming that they need to see precisely what they are saying. And around Christmas 1936 Bliss had made her decision to restrict and rein-back the comings and goings of her celebrated guests. The Wildcatters out of Chicago, the mulled-up Micmacs from downtown Anville and the hooch that could raise a blister on a leather boot, were at an end, the repeal of '33 hadn't helped much either!

In the time that was to follow after Kim's 'cherished' acquisition of the Limberlost during the late 70's; five card stud was rapidly becoming the new popular pursuit of the illustrious Banquet Room. Although there were always a bevie of players willing to 'take a flyer'; when it came down to longevity it was pretty much the selfsame trio who participated on a "marathon" basis. Formidable rogues and squanderseed wastrels of somewhat quirky disposition; all:-

For instance, take Toni Barber a big bellied Neapolitan with an immense golden heart. Why only last semester he had personally schooled Jimmy James the retard in the ebbing art of Barbermanship. At this precise moment in time Jimmy James is in out-and-out control of Toni's shop: Cutting short back and sides and even trimming the occasional beards, for the more 'assured' customers! And what of Toni himself? Well at the bumper age of 70 years, tuffet headed Toni has finally allowed himself the luxury of becoming a senior at last.

Only when the gamesters were in session, and it was past 11 in the pm did Toni feel that it was appropriate to finally let his hair down; so to speak!

Well leastways to remove his 'Elvis' rug, place it on one knee and give it a good brush, before conceitedly placing it securely back upon his near buck naked head!

Occasionally during those 'men' evenings Kim would sit quietly

25

upon the leather chesterfield in the corner of the Banquet Room and take up her knitting. She loved listening into the verbal exchanges and didn't really give a 'Godamn' if 'that' word or others were used in excess, as long as they were spoken in a quiet respectful way!

Sat there in her corner, for Kim there was no one on earth worth envying and nothing on earth that she desired to possess other than what she already had been blessed with.

Once in awhile 'her' Sandra would telephone from Manhattan, and the game would temporarily take an unscheduled breather, whilst the telephone was passed around the table so everyone can say something.

Pretty much immediately after midnight chimes was Kim's prompt to retire to her bed; it was important that she was roused and respectable and the grill hot before the early morning truckers descended at around 6am.

The dulcet sound of Kim's bedstead squeaking as she comfied down was the predeterminer to an evening of chowderheaded banter; now it could really begin in earnest!

The popular revisited question (that never had an answer) was "Lollobrigida" or "Loren"? "Clara Bow" or "Harlow"? And Bob's irritant comeback "forget the young girls, try and forget them, just be getting on with the game will you"?

George; showing caution; preferred to position his ear to Kim's bedroom door in order to double check that she was indeed asleep; and having done that, he felt it was acceptable to remove his ill sized breeches. He could now enjoy the remainder of the evening intensely relieved in his long red Randolph Scott Long johns!

The problem was that George didn't own a belt long enough to accommodate his belly; and suspenders were not the answer; in any event they were uncomfortable and he hadn't wore suspenders since second grade, or any other grade for that matter!

George was waiting patiently this particular evening to acquaint his close friends with his peachy announcement. Just several hours ago he had been "intimidated" into overdue retirement by the unexpected virtuosity of "Mr Greenback"; a whole bunch of them; even enough to choke a donkey on!

It seems as though 'Howards Hotels' or some such, had designs on Georges real estate, and the nifty Greek had allowed them to cross his leathery palms with their silver!

Not many days later after George's news had gotten out; his former wife began telephoning in a swivet "She got my answering machine every time, lucky eh!" "Says she longs for the old days back again, but wishes don't come true do they; and it's a good thing they don't! George had placed the last of his chickens in the back of his truck and felt a little pain in his chest as he straightened up. "What lasts is what you start out with" he thought "and I sure didn't start out with her!"

And what of the discombobulated Bob? Well it was true that Bob had suffered from some wickedness in his past, but whatever it was that he had to endure he would seem to have forgotten about it, at least that was the impression he gave. If quizzed he would give a teeded smile and reel of the Spock to Kirk Speech "we've sustained damage Captain, but we are still able to manoeuvre!" Dependent upon how congenial a mood he was in, sometimes he would follow his Spock speech with that Irish Folk tune, the one that goes "Napoleon and his bonnie bunch of roses oh!" The tune obviously meant something to Bob; however your guess is as good as mine!

Although Bob was the most positively quiet and retiring individual, there were times when the sheer perversity of his attitude could be kind of unsettling. He was a rather bear like, large torsoed muscular type of guy who it wasn't worth taking a chance to mess with!

Bob would never put much breath into the telling and retelling of stretched accounts of his past life; although some tittle-tattle on the street says he killed a man in a brawl several years past, at a place called Hellhole Marshes. For the most part Bob would laze back on his chair quietly and serenely through every game, passing his cards to and fro, cigarette idly dangling from the corner of his mouth. It was this prolonged quietude that tended to make folks more attentive than usual when at last Bob decided to comment on something, you just had an inclination that he had been pondering about it for some time and therefore you should be attentive.

A typical example is; on one occasion Bob had said zero all night, until without warning at around 3am he enquired "who can name the Marx Brothers?"

Catching Tony and George off-guard and unprepared and not giving them the opportunity to respond he replied "Groucho, Harpo, Chico and Zeppo. And then condescendingly he drifted away back into his coma again.

Just last week Kim had taken Bob's child under her wing and carefully tended the youngsters appalling 'polka-dots', her mother's handed down remedy of carbonate of soda and boracic ointment seemed to do the trick more than commendably. Kim's mother was an excellent quack medic, and so was Kim. Bob was ever so appreciative, not with so many words of course; but you could tell by the loosened look of his brow, that said it entirely!

It also transpired that the youngster has landed a Saturday waiting table job, someday soon when the spots had lessened some!

And so there you have it, the semi-lucid trailer of the infamous Banquet Room. It humbly arrived in the closing years of the 19[th]Century, undistinguished and insignificant, and before the 20th Century had disrobed it had become the swanky and regaling master of all ceremonies.

And now, not regretfully, its hallowed walls are slowly moving from afternoon to evening, its luxuriant walls, not mournfully have moved from evening into night. For better or worse it really does not matter, that's just the way it is. There is not a lot of point to making speeches or for a ceremonious placard adorning the walls; when events are reaching their coda sentimental pomp only exemplifies that those inevitable events are going to lose in the end.

It is only when the dead persevere that they can eventually reach the consciousness of the living, and into our dishevelled room they come alone, through littered alleyways of time, where every past encounter has become an 'old' face in a manic mirror. A mirror which is our gift to them; a mirror which has the ability to resonate its fondest regards; even though the most rugged winds of change have gone, they come again and again and some remain.

However, it's for sure that no one ever drew an unhappy hand (hypothetically or otherwise) in that long-renowned Banquet

Room.

Greed had never really got the better of anyone's mindset for very long. And therefore it is not inconceivable that goodly memories have outgrown the gloomy, if we wish to believe it, perhaps it also makes it so.

Be all that as it may, it is definitely true that the pistol has long since been substituted by the indignatious pirouetting forefinger of the here and now inheritors. And for all their sins fifteen minutes or so of 'extra' time has been called in recognition of them being such long-standing house-sitters: indeed, the deadpan density of Bob, the altruism of tenacious Toni and the downright doughtiness of genial 'rich' George is especially recondite to some folk. Those ancient squinty eyes and twitching cheeks, their fidgety backsides upon searing suffering seating. Forever fretful of the thirteen straight seconds it would take to lose it all; yet secretively contented to break even at the end of the game.

That is all any of them ever really sought after was to break even in the end, none of these ragged rascals possessed an ice-floe for a heart! Merely a kinship of spendthrift crankiness and an endearment for one another that outruns and outsmarts even the timekeeper of destiny, that is all and that is everything!

CHAPTER VIII

'Adieu'

It was a bad day for new brides, very few angels were singing, or dogs baying for that matter; but why should she care, this rose was not searching for a similar sunrise any longer. She was seeking something new, more intense, something unknown, perhaps more profound, who knows?

It was wintertime again and it seemed as though this time all the colour in the world had retreated and disappeared forever, or at least for a very long time. Every single thing had become either black or white: the ever so endless sky, a sombre faded white, a startled bird transformed to black; as though by Gods adversary. Even the happy waters in Winter Creek had turned grey with age and were seemingly becoming drunk on its own mournfulness. The silence in Anville memorial park was sombre, blanched and impassive, perhaps in the way it should be and yet it shouldn't be so quite as much as it is!

She pulled gently but firmly on the leathern reins and turned the whimpering horse toward its snug home; he gives his harness bells a frothy shake, bites the bit and trundles down the track through the old corral to his stabling.

The north wind was gathering up mercilessly as she trudged toward the family home; it seemed to be speaking to her like an unidentifiable voice – blowing through the folds of her cloths. Blowing and whispering; rigorously removing the snow and abandoned leaves from her hair and overcoat, and systematically depositing them back onto her once again.

But for Bliss her wind of bitterness had blown it's worn out best; her eyes had become adjusted to the windstorm and were not frightened anymore. The long hours that had made the darkness more apparent had finally taken leave and right now what troubled her the most was her lack of being troubled, instead of waiting for the end she had instead fought off that oncoming end.

Through the tinted lavender window glass (a wedding gift from Boston) Bliss could secretly see her tireless daughter gleefully playing in the parlour. And for Bliss her child was all and everything she treasured and cared for in her new life – now that Earle had gone.

CHAPTER IX

'de Profundis (an ode to Lillian)

The afternoon says:

"I'm thirsty for shadow!"

And the moon: "I want stars"

The crystal fountain asks for lips,

the wind, for sighs.

Federico Garcia Lorca

"What will you want, what will life hold for you, baby mine - what cadenzas will you ascend?"

Bliss came from a middle-class American Mason-Dixon line background, with a Canadian mother and a small-town Virginia father: although she was long home schooled and had lived in Southern Ontario most of her life. Indeed the notional sentence alluding to baby Lillian's destiny probably came from the emotional territory that Bliss had inherited from her parentage and home schooling. As a child her familial experience had been both less and more than the traditional concoction. In particular she was educated into the way of accepting other people by alternate means, in preference to the sensitivity of indifferent indoctrination. In some respects this had resulted in Bliss being a combination in nature of staunch resolve and empathic fervour. Perhaps it is enough to say that Bliss thoroughly understood how to activate a person's "buttons" and pressure points; and how to produce an intolerable combustion in the event it ever became necessary!

Perhaps it sounds somewhat clichéd to disclose that Bliss and Earle were the most redoubtable soul mates imaginable—but it isn't. Their relationship was one of uncomplicated like-mindedness in every respect; it was simply implausible to be any other way.

Supposedly they gave the impression of being the personification of 'Darby & Joan'. All of their surprises had always been planned together, except the ultimate abrupt cruel surprise. The surprise of utter silence, the surprise of feeling everything, and then nothing—like the silence of dead wood lying helpless in the leafy mould of the forest floor—moving only when it's prodded!

It was the type of day when not only Bliss but anyone else for that matter felt inclined not to go out-doors unless it was absolutely necessary. The last few stragglers were making their way homeward from work, bent forward as though weighted down, ducking doorway to doorway like frightened deer—it's amazing how a white-out can bring about the vulnerability of humankind!

It was as though all the clouds had unlocked every water-tight door in their armoury and unrestrained it emptied down diligently and evenly, seemingly covering every sidewalk, path and street in the entire world – nothing was left to chance – absolutely nothing!

Here in the snowy stillness there was an absence of reality. For Bliss the only reality was the tiny child asleep beside her, nothing else really mattered, the ill-tempered wind outside couldn't really blow away their home-made home, she would make sure of that, wouldn't she?

"My Lillian, little child from the backwater, only you and I are left, we're the only ones who remain from now on".

"You and I are like gallant graceful birds caught in the same concentric—spiralling, encircling and colliding with a wind of differents. Sleep easy baby mine, when you awaken, you will be bright, happy and virtuous for all time". My heart has endless spaces for you to spin"

Bliss knew that her time with Earle had been the first act only, a warm-up, and now the important second act with Lillian would be her tour-de-force number. The silent snail had become the chirping grasshopper, there was an adjustment to make and she was not the sole consideration it was as though she had been able to eavesdrop upon Lillian's dreams and now Bliss had learned to sleep the identical sleep as her child would.

The snow was beginning to sift through the weather-beaten splits of the parlour door, leaving its soft-powdered traces upon the thick woven rug: not in an obnoxious manor, more like an affable snake who had decided to shed its skin en-route.

It was a silent night for Bliss and Lillian an enjoyable silence made precisely for thoughts and dreams. And although an adult dream crept into Bliss's dreamscape regarding financial matters it was not too intense. In any event, what the hell, she would do whatever it took to provide for her Lillian, she would bear it all, whatever it took, even swindle God if necessary!

The storm of the previous day had died away and as Bliss stoked up the last embers of the dwindling fire she whispered resolutely under her breath "Anything goes for us, now that everything has gone!"

CHAPTER X

"Beginnings"

There was more than a sense of theatrical about this young woman in the cotton gingham dress, straw hat, and less than common-sense ruby walking shoes.

Perhaps it was all the fault of the first ever movie she saw; the magical magnificent rainbow- hued Wizard of Oz, such a contrast to the drabness of Anville: Full-fledged cyclones, trees and people floating in the air and midgets and flying monkeys, she just had to adore it.

Lillian was approaching twenty six; eight year older than Judy and a lot older than Dorothy, but what does that matter, marmalade and oysters may not complement one another but they are good for your soul if you enjoy them.

It had become her time of life to fill out a bit and she was beginning to have the beginnings of a little pot, although it was her so-called 'anorexic' ankles that she was mainly self-conscious about, to the extent that wearing three pairs of woollen socks in order to pad out her calves was the norm!

Lillian had always been quite strict with herself and even as a child it had never been Bliss's requirement to offer her advice; it was as though Lillian knew that certain procedures were hers alone to take care of; they were her property and nobody else's concern. Despite her day dreamy disposition at times, she never missed a single opportunity to improve her academic enlightenment, no matter how complicated the subject matter was. 'Milquetoasts' would rankle her; it was as though she had no understanding of their psyche and didn't feel obliged to learn.

From an early age Bliss had told her, "if you can't get it right the first time, it's not the end of the world, remember that you can't fail in life unless you quit!"

Whilst most of her school friends had got married and settled down, Lillian preferred to be something of a Bohemian—Like my father was; oh, he has a lot to answer for!"

It had always been Bliss's hopeful dream and assumption that at a certain "befitting moment" (when her own youthfulness was declining) Lillian would step-up and become straw boss and maitre d' of Limberlost.

However Lillian had other inclinations, she wanted to investigate city life.

On a bright Monday morning in July Lillian and her old school pal Gloria excitably opened up a beauty shop in Hamilton, in an old taxi office at Barton & Wentworth. Gloria chickened out, and only stayed six months after some local hoodlums began shaking down the more prosperous shopkeepers and restaurateurs in the community.

Bliss had been keeping her eye on events in a kind of hush-hush manner and had become kind of nettled. Bliss had some old connections and uncollected favours in Montreal and it wasn't long after Gloria left that things calmed down at Barton & Wentworth, at least they did for Lillian!

There were whispers that Carmine Galante came up from Miami, but perhaps that was just wishful thinking.

Howsoever Lillian only lasted another three years in the city, but it was her choice; "I didn't like city life, it was so completely different for me, I had to ride a bus twice every day; people shove you on busses!"

And so after some adventures Lillian returned home, almost precisely at the certain "befitting moment" that Bliss had her dreams about.

I guess that Bliss knew she was 'just coasting' of late and her always right hunch was telling her that her time was coming near to the end of the line at last.

CHAPTER XI
Raison d'etre (reason for being)

Of course, everyone owes their existence to their parents, but in Lillian's instance we must subtract one parent and add one in number, Polish Freedom Fighter.

Without whose especial intervention Lillian would never have existed and the Limberlost as we know it may have taken on a completely different persona.

Renek was a handsome man but it was the surprising maturity of his youth that particularly appealed to Bliss; he was just beyond twenty years of age. An old head on young shoulders was what she was needful of.

She did especially like his voice though. He was an excellent singer of the most beautiful romantic and sentimental ballads, and even though she didn't understand the words he would convey the words with gestures and such an immense universal warmth.

In spite of the fact that Bliss spoke two languages, Polish was not one of them and English was not one of his, however it somehow didn't really matter.

All that really mattered was whether he had enough money to

pay for his lodgings and the fact that she had been without a man for twelve years since. And even if he couldn't pay for his lodging, in any event it wasn't much of a room that he occupied – what with the cracked jug and water basin and the loosely fitted window frame that whistled like a railway engine crossing through to Buffalo.

The only disapproval that Bliss had about Renek was his appalling choice of clothing. Every day he would turn out in the most colourful traditional Polish troubadour attire. She found it kind of nerve-racking at early morning breakfast, and in any event his choice of clothes were far too risqué in this neck of the woods!

After they became lovers the out-and-out temerity of his dress really became an issue, Bliss became almost obsessively fussy and finally decided for them to pay a visit to Messrs Jacob Fuld & Partner-the most bespoke tailor in Hamilton, Ontario;

Jacob was also her Godfather and had served her father when he was alive. It just seemed right to Bliss that if Renek was to become her lover then in return he would be obliged to look like a proper gentleman!

It was a sight to behold when Renek, emerged soberly suited in 'blissful' blue, which he was instructed to wear with a white or pale blue shirt and a reticently striped tie!

In some respects their assumptions of decorousness were so mismatched, he was the natural born Bohemian, an artist of very easygoing disposition, and Bliss, at times, could be the complete bourgeois personified!

However despite their fundamental eccentricities they were happy together and that was the be-all and end-all of what really mattered to them both.

Unfortunately the only single thing that a person can be certain of in this unsuspecting topsy-turvy life of ours is that everything runs its course, and alas, that was the way it was with Bliss and Renek. He was the man that she had dreamed of finding, the friend who never was, he almost transcended gender for her. And yet one hateful and beautiful spring morning when each and every bird should be rejoicing, he was gone, disappearing like the snow that had brought him. In spite of her prayers he was not going to miraculously return, this was going to be one of those occasions when God preferred to be deceptively deaf; and she understood that her double-dealing infidelity was a smear to Earle's memory, and that was the reason why for her it happened. Suddenly she had difficulty with dignifying the twenty year disparity between their ages; she had like to convince herself that the imbalance didn't matter a hoot, but it did, it really did!

And now every guilty thought reminded her of that. No more the winning smile, the hasty song, of hearts leaping in darkened rooms.

No more the wild young man who talked too quickly and too loud. No more of the love he owned and wished to give away – or was it all just an elaborate farcical charade of good intentions versus loneliness?

Bliss felt sure that she could not endure another repetitious summer alone, not to mention another raw insipid winter. It was as though every element of her fortitude had become threadbare. All she could see were voids that can only be seen completely and for what they are, after victory over them has been achieved.

The moonrise and the sunfall, the spasms of celibate communion, without wafers and wine, the scorched dreams and feverish slumber... Until two hundred and eighty days, on schedule, her water broke! And then the badness vanished; completely, utterly, wholly and entirely, never to return again.

A hank of unbleached linen (cut and plaited) a large jar of Vaseline, a bottle of Lysol and a new enamel saucepan is all it took to dissipate her neurosis and deliver the most profound glorious legacy to her.

There are some wounds which rarely (if ever) speak out when they occur, or for that matter in the subsequent affecting years.

44

And likewise it was with Bliss.

When her sole 'reason for being' was taken during the very same inhospitable winter as her Earle, Bliss felt as though every just desert had been inflicted upon her but she kept halfway quiet, in public at least.

And eventually, after what seems like ten thousand evenings spent listening to those small consumptive cry's of the night, Bliss had her 'reason for being' returned to her; for good, once and for all; just the way that Bliss had prayed it would be, that was the way it all worked out for her.

CHAPTER XII

Also Known As...

For quite a while now Lillian has been busy transforming her priorities from the old 'good enough' way to a new here and now way.

Things that used to be important to her are now becoming inconsequentially neither here nor there. For example, whilst she still contemplates upon nylons, sodas, jukeboxes and drive-ins they 'are' just contemplation and not the be all and end all of her life, like they once were.

It could be said that perhaps Lillian's way of life has become more meaningful and abiding than it ever used to be, perhaps even a little profound in nature of late.

The upside of it all is that she has unmistakably gained a new type of continuity in her life, and that continuity has in turn helped her to feel far more relaxed and good about herself.

It's hard to believe that the once doleful face that greeted customers as they came in the door has been replaced by such a new gregarious Lillian! She just cannot wait to get behind that dairy bar and begin working her hostess routine.

It's almost as though she has become today's 'Special'. Lillian is purely and simply like an unputdownable book, Snow White's kiss and an early Christmas gift all rolled into one; rejoicing and ebullient under her flawless makeup like a princess in her very own castle.

Lillian knew, without question or doubt that everything was going to plan, and that she was behaving in precisely the manner that Bliss would have been proud of. To some extent it had always been Bliss's abstract; however Lillian had more than adequately learned the whole drill off by heart.

There had been an extraordinary reversibility of their body and soul since Bliss had gone; the type of reversibility that can only be achieved through intuitive inborn intimacy. No more Lincolnlike and lonely for Lillian, Bliss would not have wanted that for her little girl.

Leafy winds had begun to blow chilly for early September, and rich carpets of red leafiness like new enigmatic blood lay inoffensively everywhere.

Limberlost, completely unattached from the whole mind-blowing miracle of autumn splendour, just bathed itself as though the whole caboodle was just run-of-the-mill.

It was still reasonably early in the am and the rural mail carrier stopped briefly opposite the restaurant at the box labelled 'Bliss & Earle Carmen': It may sound peculiar but it had been an old observance in Anville for many years to keep the name on the box of the very first persons who had build on the land; it was as a kind and respectful gesture to them.

Lillian was up and about early as usual and was out picking and gathering in her dewy garden to her heart's content: a preparation of carrots and parsley, some parsnips and onions, and an extra large old turnip green. There was much more than a deep peace running through her rural mind that morning, as she stood-up, stretched and looked skyward. Her watchfulness was drawn toward a lingering, seething black cloud of smoke which was moving ever so quickly up toward the west. It was becoming denser by the second and seemed to be almost sporadically splintering the early rays of the autumn sun and splaying them into all directions. There are certain things in life that are so evident to you that you don't need a crystal ball to know what's going down. This was one of those occasions when no matter how quick-witted a person is, from the onset the realisation will be that they have not been quick-witted enough. Unfastening her apron and throwing it to the ground, Lillian rushed toward her vehicle and headlonged toward Anville.

Lillian's roots were infinitely embedded in her 'hick' town and even the devil himself could not be more indefatigable than she was at this daunting yet crucial intervention in time.

Without passion or reproach, there honest-to-goodness was absolutely nobody who could have done more to save those timber framed homes from destruction. The fire department chief's opinion was that perhaps we should be grateful that no lives were lost. He was right of course although some folks were quietly close to not caring, about their lives that is.

By late in the pm, when normally folks would be thinking about supper, the full extent of the fire unveiled itself. Like sickening scissors the blaze had cut Anville in two, scissors that advanced so silently and serenely until crescendoing and obliterating every tenement home on the south side of the main drag. Life had gone so well in Anville, prior to the Great Fire of '49'.

There are occasions when overwhelming bitter consequences are so immediate and so unsympathetic that even crying seems unimportant; and this was one of those occasions. Folks were almost philosophical as they shuffled and searched through the amputated debris of their homes; trying to find and snatch some small fragment of their previous lives from the blackened leukaemia of despair. Tears of tar staining their faces, dogged endurance sheltering the blows of the forge.

Anville had become a seashell which had lost its endearing echo; as hushed and inaudible as the blankets of ash upon the altar of the burnt out community mission.

Lillian fought back the floods of tears that were anxiously waiting to flow, perhaps it was the residue of hell-fire in the atmosphere or perhaps it was because she knew what her thoughts and secret wishes were. Bliss had warned her to always be cautious of emotional involvement "when you have the power to influence events, it is important that you remain composed".

Bliss spoke from experience; she had an address list of many long-forgotten names to prove it!

Lillian felt outside of herself, looking back at herself in a kind of double-act amazement; her eyes began to steal away from the obvious deceasement and look toward a viable resolve. And when she became as certain as a centipede with all its systems working that her thoughts were on track, she reined in all the homeless families:

"If you've heard of any alternatives to what I suggest then let me know – all of us have met over and over so we're not strangers and there's a truth that dwells between us and so with that in mind there's a home for you all as long as you need up on highway 21, there's plenty of room for all of you and your families".

Her young legs felt kind of wobbly as they convoyed out toward Limberlost; "and old head on young shoulders" is what Bliss would have said.

Morning broke clear today, no clouds, just a normal cold clear September day. The rural mail carrier stopped briefly to deliver The Spectator'. There was an excellent headline "Southside - Mom" and quite a passionate story from the columnist Paul G Jones, always the writer of hackneyed phrases but in this instance there were no interviewees gushing plaintively from his front page, well not too many! Most would-be interviewees were tucked-in safe and unencumbered in "Moms" complimentary cabins, and they couldn't give a hoot about an ending to the Spectator story, they knew that events were ending happily for them and so that's all that really mattered!

With regard to Lillian's take on it all, that was just a simplistic uncomplication, when being faced by the plight of her friends being buffeted around like lost kites; she had just pulled them in and pulled it off. That's what had affected her actions, nothing more or less.

The following day passed entirely productively for everyone. The 'new' residents were starting to settle in nicely and had mostly been to and froing town in order to collect a whole hodgepodge of items that they were going to require.

The townsfolk that had been relatively unaffected by the fire, had mobilized and kicked in a whole bundle of paraphernalia, including fabric, clothing and foodstuffs.

The restaurant remained open as usual and all the activity in and around the cabins had aroused interest from the customers, which prompted Lillian to start a donation appeal!

Lillian had retrieved a pair of old cribs from the encumbered attic room and between attending to customers she managed to put a lick of paint on them, two young mothers were delighted.

Some days seem to go so quickly and yet at the same time they seem so squashed full of events- such was the present day.

That evening as Lillian drifted toward untroubled sleep her thoughts could sense Bliss's melted kiss running through her soul like beautifying music; and Bliss's heart to heart words, over and again in her mind until Lillian fell asleep "Leap over those fences my sweetheart, even though you may tear your dress in doing so".

"Mom" was awake and out of her bed by six in the am. She liked to speak out loud to herself in the early AMs when there was no one else around to hear. It wasn't really anything of any sensibility that she was saying, just the same sort of old platitudes each day as an 'entree' before the main course came jangling along:

"Today I've earned the right to take things a smidgen easier and so I am just going to occupy my time with cooking and serving only" and then quietly she added "should be chopping wood and raking leaves as well!"

Tenacity and some resourcefulness is all it really ever takes to cause some small miracles to happen ... it could be that a little 'call to mind' encouragement from Bliss also helped ever such a lot!

CHAPTER XIII

Confessions!

Sandra's apartment in Manhattan, around 1982

Characters:

Sandra age 29

Dahlia - around the same age as Sandra

Jacques Leyrac age 70

Kim (Krystyna) age 43

Up on the 35th floor of her apartment Sandra gingerly answered a telephone call from the press office. A birdlike woman chattered on as Sandra gazed pensively across the East River and beyond. On clear sharp days like today the panorama was superb, and it used to amuse Sandra immensely to hear her Ukrainian housemaid enthusing over "all the sheep's on the water". It sort of gave you a nautical and rural perspective on events at the same time!

Sandra had been out enjoying the holiday weekend on her sun-deck and looked decidedly healthy and tanned, and most chicly neat in a snazzy suit of navy blue velvet.

This evening she had invited some very special friends for supper and with that in mind she had created the most sumptuous 'carte du jour' for them. For these extraordinary guests she would gladly create a whole new world of fabulous priceless things, if it were possible to do so. No amount of gratitude would ever be enough for the joys that they had given her, far more joys than her simple prayers could have asked for or imagined, let alone achieved.

From the onset Jacques had taught her so many principles and practicalities that no-one was able to defy Sandra and walk away unscathed. Jacques impressed upon her the importance of "recognizing yourself" and the simple adage that "you deserve more". From time to time he would elucidate by adding "Kim deserved more; don't sell yourself short the way she did".

In a way the whole abstraction was really something of a paradox because Jacques Leyrac was not entirely into the habit of recognizing any of his personal or business attainments in any specific way, shape or form. Although he possessed a completely self-assured nature and was certainly never slow in coming forward; in a subtle way he could also be quite self-effacing.

When Sandra first met Jacques (in her grown-up years) it struck her how cynical he was with regard to the music business and how confused he seemed to be regarding his sexual orientation. Her somewhat juvenile assessment and presumption were soon to reversibly change when by and by she discovered that Jacques lived his life under a deceptive facade. He was a unique person and his entry into her life changed everything that was needful of change and yet made her a better person for it, sometimes it was as though she was his only client that mattered. He seemed to be only interested in 'her' theatre and 'her' performances, and would lay his personal ambitions and even reputation aside to provide for it.

Indeed the chemistry between Sandra & Jacques was in a class of its own; they entered each other's life thoroughly and unconditionally and became somewhat inseparable, especially when Jacques was in town.

Similar to Jacques, Sandra was also a 'down to earth' type of individual, altogether unlike the majority of aspirant so-called artist, living their dream of figured on fame. She grew tiresome of their prancing and pasturing about with their new-found opinionated and supercilious 'talent', like a pack of overindulged kids gone amok in a candy store!

However, most of the salaried musicians in the orchestra were undeniably charming and professional. Although unfortunately by the same token they tended to be unreliable philanderers at heart and would make the worse kind of partners. What's more there was a scarcity of young interesting ladies among the musicians and therefore there was no option to make a 'nice' friend.

In any event Sandra would have sooner plumped for someone who was better suited with a slide rule than a slide trombone, or at the very least, someone with a sophisticated outlook regarding their own sexuality and was not too limited in their approach but at the same time, was not too tired and worn!

Enter Sandra's second essential guest on this uniquely remarkable evening: Her very own 'Girl Friday' Dahlia Carrière, sufficient to say that Dahlia initially was employed as Sandra's interim P.A. and had subsequently become Sandra's permanent P.A.

Lifelong that is!

Dahlia could lend her hand to practically everything in any event. She could sing, dance, act and on the occasion of Sandra's birthday she was crazy enough to tap dance down 51st in Manhattan. Having noted that, Dahlia was not in the slightest bit interested in being in show business per se. Apparently she had once given the profession a tryout and became disillusioned by show-people and their infectious take on reality, "I didn't want to be soured by the same disease" was her standby explanation.

Oftentimes Sandra had felt exactly the same way inclined. To a certain extent she had never really enjoyed seeing herself portrayed through other people's eyes, and for a considerable time her exacting acknowledgement had been that she didn't want to go on pretending an untruth. Sandra had pretty much decided that she also wanted out of show business. The hopeful anticipation this evening was that perhaps her 'haute cuisine' would be a mellowing blend to her revelations and her future intentions, and that perhaps Jacques and Dahlia would concur with her decision. Unbeknown to everyone Jacques also had some surprise disclosures to make, and the worrying thing was he was finding it difficult to come to terms with them. It was not as though he was being indecisive, to the contrary: but not since his wife's death had Jacques felt such an unjustifiable self-reproach.

Jacques Leyrac was undeniably the doyenne of Canadian impresarios. He was the mastermind who chanced on Kim and who had gotten her first Montreal contract. She had flown down from Toronto that day to meet him; and Jacques was stood waiting on the runway at Dorval airport, probably as excited as her, but looking most deceptively cool!

He took her to a swank hotel in rue de la Montagne which was adjacent to Quartier Latin where she was to debut the following night. From the onset Jacques took care of every detail during her visit, and shielded her from the lunacy of self-indulgence, which oftentimes comes to the fore at first performances. Whilst others, members of the production were swilling champagne in the lounge bar, Jacques had organised for her to be interviewed in her suite by local radio station CKVL. Sitting in the background and dragging on his cigar in short bursts, he was also keeping an eagle eye on CKVL's interviewer!

The following evening Kim's performance lasted exactly forty minutes; that was all the time she required for her audience to fall seriously in love with her. By the time she arrived back home in Toronto some twelve hours later, word of her performance had spread like wild fire. It's phenomenal and super strange why/how in order to find superstardom an artist must absent their home town for the purpose of drawing attention to themselves back in their own home town! Perhaps that's just the way the cookie crumbles, however Jacques knew why and that all that really matters. Jacques knew that even after a lifetime in his business nothing could have prepared him for Kim, he could scarcely believe how such emotion could exist. It was as though the true art of singing had been half-forgotten or neglected for years and she had somehow revived it.

Jacques became rightly so pernickety over the types of venues offered to his prodigy.

He considered a variety theatre or nightclub way beneath her dignity. No one gave him any quarrel about it when he insisted upon her performing only in a concert hall and it being the Tchaikovsky Theatre in particular. He also insisted upon a Steinway, and that same obsessive requirement was echoed again during Sandra's staging in ensuing years. Jacques had quite a penchant for stylization!

In the early 1960's Jacques together with Quebec had moved

wholesale into the 20th Century at last. The Nation too was also changing. In 1965 the old Canadian Flag modelled on the Union Jack was replaced by the magnificent Maple Leaf Flag.

On the streets there was a quiet revolution going on, no barricades, no storming of prisons, no guillotine, but a massive and exciting social change. Jacques and his creative new bride were a pair of young intellectuals who felt obliged to challenge almost everything, until one day she unexpectedly died. And for Jacques, Quebec suddenly became an uninhabited wilderness; Seven million of its citizens just got up and disappeared; debates regarding posterity and democracy vs. dictatorships suddenly and abruptly became wasteful irrelevant piffle!

After all the tears, frowns and litanies had been responded to, and expounded, Jacques began his befuddled path out and away from the elusive answers. However his pledge to abstain from attachment was perfectly and unquestionably clear, he would never allow himself another time to become a victim!

It could therefore easily be assumed that was the reason why Jacques current friends and business acquaintances had deemed him to be a homosexual. Seeing as the majority of them belong to a generation who had not known Jacques in the 60's, and had no inkling about the tragic death of his wife. Withal, as far as they were concerned he had never been socially linked with any female whatsoever.

Jacques knew darn well that folks had speculated regarding his sexuality and his 'very' private life; he felt reasonably comfortable about the rumours and it would even give him a secret chuckle from time to time to reflect upon just how curious it was that well-meaning people can't say what they mean to say, when they think they know that you know what they know!

There had been particular occasions when to a certain extent the 'gay' slant had actually benefited his business, there were several big shots, celebs and young aspiring starlets and actresses who used his agency only because they felt at ease with him.' A perfect example was Kim, she would never had felt so relaxed and safe with her mentor and enjoyed his company so enormously, let alone agreed to share a suite together, had she had a notion that he was anything less than gay.

It would seem that no complexities exist where there is a presumed impossibility of being straight.

Jacques and Kim spent the majority of the day and into late evening perfecting the roles and new roles she must play. In the blaze of publicity she had created it was now necessary for her to tackle several outstanding parts and painstakingly recreate the characters from within. He, busy at the piano with enthusiastic encouragement, scratch pad and pencil; her, on an adventure though Rossini, Bellini and Donizetti. Her voice would have its ups and downs but even it's 'downs' would compel Jacques absolute admiration. Throughout her career Kim was able to bring a particular sensibility to the women who she played. It was a though they were all victims, as she believed she was. Oppressed like Lucia or Traviata, or avenging like Turandot or Tosca. They are the same women whether they raise the knife or offer themselves up defenceless. They are above all women in love and victims of their love.

There had become a kind of detached cool between Jacques and Kim which was kind of indicative to their contradictory denial that all was not the same between them: not actually noticing one another, yet taking notice of one another, but only just enough to not let it show to much! Perhaps it was enough (but not reason enough) to be inebriated by incessant beakers of steaming black coffee brewed in their workroom kitchenette. Perhaps the reason enough was more intrinsic in nature to being the cause, and when it takes the midnight snow to blow away the cobwebs of rehearsal and the fireplace aglow to warm cold feet and hot rum in an empty tum to bring excitement of it all happening again tomorrow, then that is indeed reason enough; and all it requires!

There is a somewhat clinical term called 'evolving', well in any event it is the point where two friends brought together by inappropriately named 'fate', suddenly find themselves in the realm of one person.

It happens so diligently and so evenly that it is just as though it had always been this way, like somehow they had always been this dependent upon each other. Predictably and also unpredictably like new born infatuated butterflies; shoulder to shoulder, no longer finding it necessary to keep their distance; finding their way to extraordinary immortality together without the need for logical direction any longer.

Every sharp edge of edgy apprehensive disposition and hesitant doubt perfectly melted away.

No thoughts of disappointment, no reason for accountability in a predestined world, no misgivings ... well maybe!

Some people can only give what they themselves need, others barely take notice of all they are giving, Kim was in the latter.

The journey she was taking with Jacque was for her like a journey into an out and out unknown. It was an emotional and tempestuous journey, a complicated passage where such sentiments of the heart can dominate and reshape all reason. Indeed it had made Kim become increasingly more vulnerable; on stage and off stage she was no longer the same characterised renowned female singer round whom everything revolved.

The awful truth had become sorrowfully obvious to Jacques. He remembered so vividly all her early recordings, of how she had reached the top and stunned the world. But she was a star even without records.

He recalled that often as the curtain went up, merely her sudden emergence onstage would provoke some onlookers in the audience to unexpectant tears, before she uttered a note.

The complication of late was that she was losing her waifish look and fevered capability, it was as though she had become more relaxed and her music almost 'sweet-sounding'. The former 'Kim' had been carelessly shoved into storage because she was no longer necessary. Her surreal suffering had given her fame and become a self-full filling reason for her sell out success and now it was her new phlegmaticness that was destroying her.

Jacques dearly wanted themselves to be the selfsame reborn soulmates for good and for all time, he wanted it to mean the same today as it did yesterday; but her love for him was far too high a price to impose upon her.

Jacques used his 'gay' wildcard, it was the only card he could play without her being the loser, and so that's the way it had to be.

It seems odd that when sacrifices have been made at such an astute level, that there is no fanfare to follow, or even a ceremonial pat on the back or handshake. When she left that evening all that remained was a vacuum of emptiness and a grave like silence. 'Leastways she is free if all goes well'; Jacque was mistaken!

All did not go well: Kim's air was filled with songs and music by bad maladroit amateurs whose business it was to line their own pockets. Living at fever pitch, eventually like any adrift star, she tragically burnt herself out.

But times and circumstances can change people, and sometimes even sadness can be happiness in its disguise; and it is almost certain that the something that makes a person so sad; at one amazing time made that same person really happy. It may be an inevitability not to experience some degree of sadness by admitting to being profoundly in love; and perhaps that sickening sadness is an opportunity to become learned about the unresolved love and not to make so many wild guesses about it.

In any event, and without question, as far as Jacques was concerned, Kim may not possess a kingdom any longer but she was still his queen. And as far as Kim was concerned there was no right or wrong in Jacques deception and she no longer felt any misery for not being loved; however she did feel a little grouchy from time to time for wanting to love him.

And so there we have it: Devilish Dahlia in an amazingly ill-cut garland dress: stylistic Sandra the pizzazz pianist that Dahlia 'hits it off' with, and street wise Jacques in a Gatsby suit straight out of Fitzgerald's novel.

You would imagine that Central Park would be a relatively safe place to take a quiet leisurely meander on a Sunday afternoon; be that as it may but there is no accountable explanation why a 'Time Out' reporter found Kim's "present but not to be seen as present" request somewhat curious? It would seem quite clear that her presence can still perfume a room or indeed a park!

CHAPTER XIV

Conclusions

On the same day that the New York Post blazoned their front page with news adjudging Kim's marriage to her "ancient impresario", Sandra left her apartment to buy a newspaper. At the nearby news-stand a grey-haired man was busy scrutinizing the headline, and as Sandra arrived he cynically announced to the world in general "yet another youngster has got herself conveniently hitched to a geriatric" Sandra smiled at the man's naivety and uninformed awareness, and secretly wondered what awful complimentary criticisms would be aimed at her, and banded around town when her relationship with Dahlia was finally revealed! Whether its Deans double vision, Sinatra's aging treble or Phyllis Diller's breasts, the press are never lost for a few ideas of what to do with a bombshell and metaphor or two!

As for Kim and Jacques they can easily be ranked with Scarlett, Rhett and many other semi- precarious Latter-Day Saints. And in any event their type of loneliness was never going to be alleviated by applause of any number of crowds or clientele. As far as Kim and Jacques were concerned the cool pre-winter sun was perfect in Montreal. Even when they couldn't see it, they were Lucky enough to still be extremely warm and contended. And that's all that mattered to them.

It's curious and incredible magical how dreams can oftentimes come to the surface and run into reality, and how in turn reality can dissolve completely into dream; it's all just a matter of time, like it was for Kim and Jacques.

Being with Dahlia Carrière was kind of like eating bananas backstage with Carmen Miranda. If she told you they were amazingly delicious, then you had no choice but to ask for more. On the other hand if she decided to get rid of them because they were boring and quite ridiculous, you would be obliged to move heaven and earth to gratify her desire that is precisely the way it is; being with Dahlia Carrière!

Undeniably, being an "item" was never a "to be or not to be" question, it was merely an educated assumption of the inevitable truth of the matter. For example when Sandra enquired "why do you love me", Dahlias responsive comeback was "because I knew we were perfect together". And when Dahlia raised the same elucidator Sandra straight-away replied "because you like taking walks in the risqué parts of town... and I feel so safe with you."

Oftentimes that's all it takes, it really doesn't need to be a profound set of words or events to see things in black and white, or even to become aware that something altogether spectacular is coming about. It's quite often the comparatively negligible occurrences that when put together tend to create a monumental

68

evolution. Like this morning over breakfast when they both burst into laughter over recalling the previous evening at Loews Theatre; where the ticket girl was stood behind the candy counter eating popcorn and smoking Winston! Those small incidents, oftentimes that's all it takes to harness harmony.

Sandra was smiling like a china cup over blue-white gingham today. The daughters of destiny who had taught the moon to smirk and the stars cavort were coming home. Although Dahlia had not ever visited Canada she never-the-less had an attraction to the county "because it has such beautiful scenery" and because of a picture she had seen in "Good Housekeeping!"

As for Sandra it was as though she had transcended time and was returning to the body where she was born, where her heart had remained, and all those unspeakable farewell tears had begun.

At the counter they huddled over a frothy Latte, in the depths of the Greyhound Terminal. Waiting expectantly, excitedly, exhilarantly. Sandra finger tapping the Laminate like an impatient virtuoso, Dahlia tapping her nimble toes like Adele Astaire. Unmindful of their restless gestures, uncertain of applause and thoroughly unrepentant of their decision and the resolve.

They had outshone this amazing city and the finale was destination homeward, back to the beginning, to repatriation and Limberlost.

George was wearing a "brand-new" white jacket from Anvilles illustrious thrift shop. With his curly black hair well slicked down with that "greasy kids stuff" and water he really looked the bee's knees today.

Since his property was acquisitioned a while back, George had been living in an old storeroom (out the back of the restaurant) which Kim had lovingly revamped for him. George had also become Kim's sort of unofficial straw boss. Today he had been whiling away the time with his lady friend Alice, (a retired teacher of respectful disposition) the pair of them had been watching an old Jimmy Cagney movie on Channel 7. For the meantime at least George had completely lost the feelings in his right hand, 'got to hold-on to an ice beer or two through White Heat" he explained, pinching the skin back to life.

Pinder, George's muttonhead mongrel was way ahead of the oldsters. It was as though he already knew that something was going down; and he was out at the bus stop waiting for the girls and kind of making an exhibition of himself, by spasmodically kicking up earth by the road side. Alice declared that he was "just like Rin Tin Tin, pretending to find a rabbit hole or such" George nodded in agreement; whatever Alice says she is invariably right.

George strolled toward a well-used comfortable root under the wide-branched 'bus stop tree' and with Alice they wearily accommodated their venerable sterns. They looked almost imitative sitting there: the tree, George and Alice. It was as though the epochs of time had somehow turned their petals to heartwood and presently they were all patiently waiting for a hundred years of needed rest.

George did care for Alice, but he really missed his chickens more. Although he had become moderately well-to-do, he occasionally meditated on his purpose in life. He thought it was similar in nature to watching that old movie, where the last reel sometimes winds back on itself, but you really want it to finish.

Unbeknown to George, when the new mattress's have settled in they will very soon have him grinning like an old mule eating cockleburrs again!

CHAPTER XV

Immortalized Moments

Somewhere between the eastern foothills of the magnificent Rockies and the infinitely vast prairies lies the exuberant city state of Calgary. Although locales tend to change (they seldom do remain the same) invariably they tend to change for either better or for worse; rarely do they become downright indifferent. Or it may be that in Calgary's instance she had become somewhat profoundly so!

It was verging on a paradox that ever since 'young gun' Joe Burke had up-sticks and pulled-out, Calgary (as he recalled it) had metamorphosed itself into a relatively larger and positively moreso sophisticated city than it had ever dared to assume it could possibly imagine was achievable. And yet despite the influx of skyscrapers, galleries and so-called avant-garde theatres, the 'revamp' has a surprisingly double-edged disparity about the whole aesthetic shebang. Inasmuch that it has still retained an air of the frontier town it used to be, where pickup trucks and cowboy boots are not entirely out of place.

Somewhere in the neighbourhood of due east alongside where Bow River comes across Elbow River, nestles "Saucy Willow Ranch" - or leastways what remains of it!

In his early headstrong days Saucy Willow had been Joe's secret garden, his very own esoteric oasis, a place of self-realisation or where he could just unbutton and hang loose. Be that as it may, when 'black gold' came ungraciously to the region it well put paid to Joes uninhibited carte blanche way of life. "That's just the way it works out when change comes to visit". Joe had always been somewhat philosophical by nature and consequently when he was obliged to pack his grip and move-on, he was not as dismayed as you would have imagined.

However, "inevitability" habitually follows 'change' in one way or another, and of late the clamorous comings and goings were settling down; the revellers had piped all they could from the earth and skedaddled. Apart from the odd soaked patches of turf, Joe's boonies were once again returning to its normality.

The seasons had a habit of coming down savagely in this region and Joes old homestead had been bearing the brunt. The north wind that sweeps unceasingly in from the open county sometimes decides to stay a little too long: until eventually every tree and grain of soil begins to grow senescent in the backwash. The one-time regaling bunk house now shimmered-down and hushed, seemingly it had drawn (perhaps shuffled) closer to the predominate cabin, almost as though they were in cahoots! Everything about the place seemed to have grown a tiny itsy-bitsy uglier than Joe remembered things to be. Glimpsing himself pass-by an unshuttered window it suddenly came to mind that 'he' also looked overly more grizzled that he last remembered!

However none of that balderdash really mattered that much because the ulterior motive behind the current ephemeral visit was wholly and acclaimly to showcase his former home to his Lillian. It was Joe's informal way of open-handedly explaining to Lillian that there is more to his makeup than a bronco and a saddle – be it an erstwhile career.

There was no denying that Joe hadn't had his brains jerked about on numerous occasions; having said that, it was not to imply that he could easily be branded as 'bronk-drunk'. Unlike many of his 'younger' contemporaries Joe never had a twitch or a nervous disposition for that matter.

When all is said and done Joe was knowing that it was pointless to attempt to impress Lillian with doodahs and whatsits that he was unschooled and unfamiliar with.

A fine example would be an airplane excursion to Europe or a sea cruise. Joe was distrusting of the ocean, he like to be surrounded by land masses. And as for French Cuisine—it doesn't matter with which hand the fork is held, does it?" When all is said and done it is all just too restrictive for Joe!

Joe's comprehension was not one of ignorance or indifference even though it perhaps seems that way. The long and the short of it was mainly because for the most part of his life he had lived with horses. It was therefore his tendency to interpret his particularities from a whole range of unacquainted perspectives to the rest of us.

For example, like a well loved horse Joe savvied that his Lillian was more inclined (and responsive) to loving, when she was loved, whether that be a lifetime journey or merely a single summer day alone together.

What Joe didn't realise though is when it all came down to it, it was comparatively "even-steven" in these matters. For in spite of the fact that Joe knew the side of the bed that Lillian preferred; she always held the bridle and she knew exactly what it took to keep him there, they both held the secret to their secret selves that was the be all and end all of it. Nothing more or less.

Blue-jeaned and apple-cheeked, like an ageing Roy Rogers and Dale Evans astride an evergreen Trigger and Buttermilk. Both twin souls searching for that dogged tomorrow in the most largest uninhabited palace of wonder in the world, Canada.

For Joe & Lillian their married life together had transcended all its most popular definitions made them more different, more alike and perhaps a wee bit more 'portly'. In any event from Lillian's perspective she had never ever heard about or read about a beau like her Joe, for Lillian there was even an element of sexiness in just the way his paunch flowed over his belt loops. And what of Joe? He could never have supposed that he would be fortunate to stumble across a gal with their very own 1955 Cadillac Fleetwood, another 'horsepower' he was also familiar with!

When all is said and done it is the relatively simple things (not the fancy stuff) that makes each day together the best day yet. Like skipping flat stones across the lake, (it's no fun at all by yourself) or watching the horses run down the meadow and scatter (like frisky children when schools is out) and at the end of each day, watching them returning to Joes red barn slow and single file; and nosing each other as they thirst and draw in water.

Joe and Lillian enjoyed watching horses—life means the most when you're able to celebrate unconditionally.

Morning broke clear today, no fog, no rain, just a perfect clean crisp September morning that reassures all life that undoubtedly the blueprint came straight from God. Descriptive words well-nigh lacklustre in this clime and in any event there are hardly enough superfluities in the universe that can devour your inhalation like the hungriness of pure-bred air.

That previous evening they'd laughed and leg-pulled over the complete shambles of Joe's cabin. The cranky mattress that answered back with every love, the mouldy window glass with two hearts inscribed upon it. The whole evening was sidelined by humour and it wasn't until next morning, mute and mesmerized by tiredness, that they discovered the significance of their 'hoedown'. The first night in their first home, a picture of immortalised moments; a 'cause' to hang-on to and keep.

Bogart, Gable, Monroe and Jimmy Dean they all gave us immortalised moments, although not in their lifetimes. Perhaps because there are as many pathways leading away from those 'special' moments as there are pathways leading to them. Perhaps immortalised moments so need to be recognised and stared straight in the eyes, or be lost for all time.

It is similar to a band of geese they spotted on that especial early morning: flying in or back from somewhere to where the winter will be less hard.

Just customary routine for the geese, but for those mavericks that 'recognise' the event, such as Joe and Lillian, it was an honoured and enduring ephemeral moment: Immortalised in their minds for all time.

And there, just above the trees another band of birds begin bringing up the rear, like a vanguard keeping guard on the first band; like a victory sign across the sky to their supporters.

Conceivably, it doesn't have to be a comet falling from the sky to bring about an immortalised event. The 'cause' can be as imagined as La Mancha's fiesta.

It's possible that, all that is required is Don Quixote's enthusiasm!

It can be as complex or as simplistic in any particular way we see fit; and it's always going to be 'spectacular' when time-out is taken to be in love.

CHAPTER XVI
Catching some Z's!

The morning was bright and clear and threw a peculiar soft chilliness rippling across the ochre sheeted landscape! Wispy scuffles of rich fallen leaves rolled nonchalantly over the dying tuffs of mimosa-hued grass toward the surety of another harsh wintertime. The expectant birds that had waited so patiently on the stoop to be fed (with leftover croissants) eventually grew tired of waiting and headed off skyward.

Jacques awakened, tarrying with the afterglow of melodic music dreamily running through his mind. Who was it singing solo? Perhaps Jeanette MacDonald, perhaps his Kim? It was puzzling at this time of day to decide whichever – although the accompaniment of apple blossoms was explicit enough to distinguish!

He fumbled carefully across sleepy Kim to the bedside bureau for a cigarette; but sadly remembered they'd finished the last one together the evening before. "The hell with those cancer sticks; who needs them?" he cogitated exonerating himself – Kim was every bit of adrenalin rush he had ever desired.

It was as though there was a divine magnetism taking place when she took him in her gaze. He could, in a twinkling of her eyes become Kirk Douglas, Burt Lancaster and almost every other tough guy he had seen at the Plaza Theatre in Montreal. Be it an ever so ridiculous performance, (for an ageing Svengali) Kim could make him roll an 'L' like Bogart or swagger like big John Wayne: and he became downright 'dangerous' after a bourbon or two!

After the premature loss of his first love, Jacques' heartache had intensified; his period of mourning where he could languish and grieve had become a sustenance to him. He became unbearably disenchanted and cynical and was motivated purely by his self-perpetuating pity; and his business activities. As far as Jacques was concerned there never was any so-called 'master plan' that existed – "life is random and events will always have the knack of turning out just the way you least expect them to". And with regard to love; "so much of nothing is passed off and praised as 'true love' and yet when all is said and done the reality of 'true love' is merely an idealized illusion of the truth". At least that is the way that Jacques used to see it; from his prospective at that time.

However, when a comet comes out of nowhere before the twelfth night passes; and dreams you've long forgotten to dream become resurrected and factual; and when even her legs give the impression of being a lot longer than they used to be – that is the moment when the negativity of yesteryears' musings rapidly become apparent!

And what of Kim? In the bad old days it was as though her whole life had been written out for her in lower case and from time to time she had been allowed a punctuation by a very occasional "exciting" semicolon. "For a very long time I thought I was dead Jacques – I thought I'd lost my life but you found me and I got it back". Be that as it may, it was Jacques who provided her with a redoubtable full-stop and, what is more, a newfangled paragraph indented clearly to each serving of her life – and that was all and everything she had yearned for.

The mutual history of their past had finally been exonerated: the consequence of regrets quashed, questions replied to and given rationality. They had met each other and themselves coming around for the second time, whereas before they merely passed-by, on this occasion they touched: and found the thing that's hardest to find – themselves! Theirs was a beautiful sickness, the type of sickness that brings about reassurance, and with that reassurance; contentment. The type of persuasive sickness that insists bed is a nice place to be; until noon! And the type that fearfully suggests there may never be another tomorrow; and for that reason it also suggest the importance of non-stop chit-chat – mandatory whilst the going is good!

Kim awakened with a pessimistic afterglow belonging to E.J. Prats "Come Not the Seasons Here" running chillingly quiet through her dreamy mind.

Jacques propped himself on one arm and gazed endearingly into her demure sleepy face. Instinctively she took him in her devoted arms; finally and forever there would be no one else.

If a love-in dictates a missed breakfast, hey, no hassle – it's far healthier than a missed opportunity; and in any event the kitchen can be a free-for-all later. It's not going anywhere soon!

CHAPTER XVII

The Reunion

It was around early evening during the late December 1989 when Kim and Jacques Leyrac made their somewhat ostentatious entrance at Montreal's Ritz-Charlton Hotel.

She looked strikingly beautiful wearing a short, close-fitting evening dress of matt satin with a slender black velvet belt: the neck-line was square and modest with narrow straps. Around her shoulders she wore a stole of the same material and was luxuriously adorned with a simulated chinchilla grey fur coat. Kim Leyrac's slim golden wedding band upon her finger was made ever so eye-catching by the complete absence of other elaborate accessories.

There was little doubt; she was an innate conspicuously clear-cut 1960's lady who second-guessed the nauseous 1980's with the belief that there is no known substitute for quality couturier and that ebullience is somewhat timeless. And very proudly on her arm; Jacques Leyrac – suitably attired in his best bib and tucker (and feeling pride and satisfaction in his own achievements and those of this wife – which really amounted to the same!) The advent being the celebration of their first wedding anniversary and that being the case, it didn't come any better than dining and carousing at the famous Ritz-Carlton!

There became several apologetically punctuated interludes throughout each stage of their meal: perhaps every thirty minutes or so. A muddled note, a long written message, an international telegram, or two – testaments of laudation addressed to the 'seemingly' last heroine of North American opera. Finally, the 'piece de resistance' by a mega charming maitre d' hotel – a nosegay of multicoloured roses presented with a respectful bow! Kim raised her glass in salute "for all the quiet you've brought into my life – thank you Jacques.

An eager fresh-faced reporter hesitantly pursued them as they sauntered hand-in-hand casually across the emptying restaurant toward the Lounge Bar. During her return to her adopted Montreal, the press had been so-inclined to pile superlative on superlative upon her – effectively in their 'qualified' estimation she could do no wrong!

"We all love you passionately Kim" he graciously blurted. Followed by a polite and appropriate "what are your plans for the future Kim – can we expect one more performance at the Metropol?" Before responding, she first glanced toward Jacques – as though he was the 'grown-up' and in a mischievous spontaneity of childishness, she replied "I am going to be an ordinary woman – with children, a home..."looking somewhat knowingly bewildered she added "and a dog; a poodle, I think!"

Kim had wished a little too much in her past life; she never had envisaged that her 'tour-de-force' lifestyle would comprise of those sometimes girlish wishes. The years of vicissitudes, during which she had come to know just as many musical triumphs as personal defeats, were all power for the course to her.

No prima donna in the world had even come close to attaining such dramatic notoriety. Although her explosive voice had gone through its tantrums and changes people just did not argue about her voice anymore. They simply knew it, recognised it and understood it – with all of its subtleties and its limitations, her voice had still managed to defy description.

Today Kim's head was as clear as high hill air on a bountiful spring morning, she knew (almost!) faultlessly what precisely her needs strained to be.

She gave the young reporter's hand an affectionate squeeze which left him kind of mesmerized and bemused – in verbatim to every other over-enthusiastic audience member all over North America.

Kim perched her 'non-existent' derrière upon the tallest bar stool she could find, like a linnet on a limb – she needed to peer straight into Jacques' eyes "ask my name Jacques, it's yours – you gave it to me. Demand my purpose Jacques, it's you; you gave me that purpose. Disentangle me Jacques, my needs are only those wants that you also want and nothing more besides". Jacques contemplated her beautiful face seriously and knowingly. She was indeed the summertime of his life: on record, on stage or personally she was his diva, his heroine or anybody that he had ever imagined. She could play each role to the full, right down to the very last insignificant word – hers was an unblemished aria of unconditional exquisiteness.

However, although her private life still maintained the capability to make the newspapers, there were, nevertheless, fewer press stories about her of late. At times, it would seem that the curtains had very nearly all fallen upon her particular metier.

On account of which is why Jacques had precariously tiptoed to the telephone whilst Kim was preoccupied in the huge bubble bath he had arranged for her earlier this morning.

Norma, Traviata, Tosca and Kim's proposed participation in such were purely 'hot-air' intimations to the press in order to rouse them up and in fact they were commonsensically totally inaccurate suggestions. Nonetheless, Jacques' pure happy-go-lucky embellishment of reality had helped enormously to enhance a great lady's evening.

It was almost as though December 31st 1989 had become a somewhat closing and conclusive recognition of Kim's supremacy. In any event, in Jacques' deduction, Kim had never been younger or more beautiful than she had tonight.

The two of them had barely arrived home and stepped into the house when there came an authoritative rapping on the front door glass panel. "I'm on my way" Jacques yelled buoyantly. A cheery mannered young fellow stood at attention in the doorway – "Western Union Sir" he blustered. Jacques signed his chitty and the youngster gave a smile as Jacques pressed some greenbacks in his hand.

"Another review Kim hey?" he called back over his shoulder. He read the telegram out loud and it was as though an iron silence was taking his tongue and causing fall out over everything. He recounted how Lillian wisecracked that "my Joe would have absolutely no idea of what to do with a metaphor if he was to find one" and now 'he' alma mater extraordinaire, had damned difficulty in communication just 16 words into a less raging sentence.

A flood of tears crowded Kim's eyes; it was as though her limbs had become swollen and she couldn't move. She held out her arms for Jacque in an unconscious effort of control. This time there was no need for speech, no need for questions of salvation – they both knew the answer and the awful realisation that the journey back to so-called normality would be longer than the forward run.

Sooner or later evening will dredge the darkness of nights into its recovery mode; and the circumstances that maimed and disfigured, just a tiny bit, begin to erase. The telegram on the table was growing older and greyer; Kim had reconciled to stammer and stutter in her sleep – and Jacques, 'bountiful mother' extraordinaire had his obligation to listen. It is just a matter of being compliant with chance in the abject culmination of events!

When a woman like Lillian succumbs to too much love; at times like this her soul will secretly long for the time when it is owed no one anything. In the end, it is as though the punishment to reach her is that of which she has reluctantly brought upon herself. Kim knew this through and through, it was all part of the unusual empathy that coupled her and Lillian. An empathy that was not only kindred but that also could be quite intense and to a certain extent, unsettling. It was a type of correlative relationship that was just incomparable to equate – as was losing Joe.

The following morning whilst Kim stared blindly at breakfast TV, Jacques wrote an editorial for 'Solo Voice' magazine. Each person feeling altogether free to undertake almost anything, whilst doing pretty much nothing. If you like, it was all part of a semi-passive action to achieve, deceive or just to become less increasingly involved – with matters of the heart.

The following evening Jacques added a cushion and positioned himself like an eagle owl on the piano chair. With elbows hanging loosely and naturally he began a soft approach to Bach's Fugue in 'A' minor – in a low plaintive voice Kim hummed along; remembering all the things that she felt had missed her attention and nothing more.

Welcome home Diamond Lil......

Midway through Jacques' Fugue there was heard an almighty fracas, pertaining to some kind of altercation at the frontage of their house, seemingly it was between a local taxi cab driver and his elderly 'caterwauling' woman passenger.

Now, Jacques had particularly chosen to settle in Old Montreal, exclusively because the populace were inclined to be of a more refined nature. Consequently, the undesirable hullabaloo at this hour of the night had really got his dander up.

Somewhere around this time, Kim had inquisitively decided to tag along and accompany Jacques on the front porch 'podium'.

"Get your mother out of my nose lady" – I've a good mind to report the old bitch" the irked-out cab driver was addressing Kim – but moreover, his ornery passenger! She never seemed to stop shrieking and most of the gist of it all seemed to be lost in translation! "Godless Kwee Beckey Polack bastard, don't even know the leer-icks to Eau Canada – when I was a rug-rat I could recite them in English, French, Canajan and Joual – what kind of patriot is he? Says he is from 'cross the border' yet he don't even know the beginning of the Gettysburg Godam Address and he can't whistle "West Side Story".

"Seems to me he could be a sneaky Commie Bolshevik fifth columnist or such – I don't guess he knows even what his dick is for!!"

Forever the diplomat, Jacques pressed a bunch of sweaty greenbacks into the astounded mouthed driver's hand and aptly expressed his profuse apologies and regrets. The consoled driver had a notion that his pride had been reconciled by the thickness of the wad. He gave Jacques a pitiful half smile and drove off mumbling "good luck man".

Mom (Lillian) was legging it up the front porch steps as though diddly-squat had happened. "Who's for crispy potato pancakes – zmarrafact, you've not tried them before have you Jacques?" Jacques had heard all about the 'adventures' of Lillian – whether they be speculation or supposition didn't really matter – she sure was some ritzy spunky lady.

Jacques poured them all a tumbler of two thirds bourbon, one third coke "stabilizer" whilst Lillian had seated herself cross-legged in the centre of the lounge. It was her stage and this was going to be some lengthy gabfest – Savoir faire Lillian!!

"Just died, right there in his sleep didn't he. Not ever did I know he was dead until hours later when he didn't drink his cocoa – I tried giving it to him on a spoon and splotched it over his new shirt".

"I really do like weddings and specially funerals but it just seemed right and proper that Joe was buried at home – at Saucy Willow Ranch. That was the way he would have wanted it".

"And so me and Ranger Mike dragged Joe up to the bluff – he was heavier than a dead minister I can tell yous"

"Ranger Mike was protesting most fiercely and was starting to get all squirrelly – he wasn't truly in favour of leaving Joe on the bluff. But I convinced him that this way Joe could keep an eye open on his land"

"In any event, Ranger Mike dug Joe a decent deep hole – weren't going to be any wild thingamajigs digging Joe up; some of them creatures would steal a soggy doughnut from a bucket of snot".

"So dears, I guess after supper I'll be making tracks back to Anville to make sure the girls are being useful, not just ornamental. And George, I've missed his craziness. I hear-tell he has taken a lady friend recently. He's so deserving of a good woman – I hope when he dies he don't die with a hard-on!"

Mom patted the chesterfield and beckoned Kim to her side "You know what they did in the old days when it rained? They let it rain! There is just no value in worrying about what you cannot control child. That type of worrying is not worth a strawberry in a bear's ass Kim; remember that!"

The evening emptied; Mom left for Anville; Kim lay in bed on Jacques' arm contemplating. "What's bugging you Kim, I'm curious?"She smiled "I just cannot get that picture of the strawberry out of my mind Jacques!

CHAPTER VIII

Impressions

It was on the last Sunday in November that Sandra and Dahlia impromtuly decided they'd like to see 'Stars of the Soviet Ballet'. Having said that, when they eventually arrived in down-town Hamilton, the theatre seats were completely sold out! So totally impulsively they purchased two bunches of chrysanthemums from a raggle-taggle street vendor (white for Sandra, purple for Dahlia) and journeyed disappointingly home.

It's really quite paradoxically wacky how/why if oftentimes turns out that "providence" can go to work in such an altra-mysterious fashion. For example, consider the date: the last Sunday in November – a date of absolutely no significance. Any yet, without the girls passing short of the Soviet Ballet it may never have become a vital element of a much bigger game plan (which, as Mom would wittingly retort "nay a fart was out of place to let it happen"). Even the credulously innocent purchase of chrysanthemums was to play an integral contribution in the final extraction of events.

Importantly, and notwithstanding that the evening had been a miserable disappointment, they were both still all gussied-up like barbers' moggies in their best Sunday-go-to-meeting clothes.

It may only be a personal observation but quite often, and to all intents and purposes, a first or a favourable impression resulting from, is also greatly significant as an ongoing impression. Even in an instance where there may have been some considerable time-lapse between the earliest 'first impression' and the current evaluation of same. Even (for that matter) where any impression at all is most probably as stage-managed and as insincere as a chorus girl's kiss is. The "much bigger game plan" is fundamentally the point at issue when all is said and done.

It was verged on late evening when Ted Waite's bus finally arrived at Limberlost and set Mom off directly at the door. It had not been part of his scheduled route; but be that as it may, his digression was more that just being personable or good-deeded would bring about. To a large extent it was owing to some improper shenanigans around 1967 which culminated with Lillian forsaking her nylons in the back seat of his Buick!

The restaurant was so serenely (and ridiculously) quiet that you could virtually hear the heavy fog lifting around the peach and pear trees.

"Jesus H. Christ, business is slower here than the second coming, it's downright doolally!" Moms first thoughts were a lot more relevant that she imagined; and her first impressions were equally so, for that matter.

She began to light her umpteenth cigarette of the day, flicked it away in distraction, and head longed hastily toward the restaurant kitchen area.

Moms unexpected appearance had caught all and sundry unawares. There were no friendly 'hi's' or buddy-buddy 'how-de-do's' she was just up in the air like a deranged avenging angel; and they knew it; or leastways it was nothing less than their first impression!

Sandra looked so unusually and exceedingly ultra cool: In a black print dress against her tanned skin and hair combed back, tight and neat. She had just finished cutting-up sorrel for vegetable soup and was taking off her apron to join Dahlia – who was sitting at the worktop eating pastrami.

Dahlia looked as pretentiously pretty as a speckled pup and was wearing those dangling type earrings. The kind that are either costing the earth or bargain-basement tack – and you can rarely distinguish which. Mom could certainly appreciate the reason why Sandra was so attached to her. At least that was Mom's first impression.

From through to the Banquet Room a clatter of plates being retrieved indicated that George and Alice had polished off their evening supper. The distinct aroma of fish and cigars indicated what they had just partaken of; and what they were doing now. Apparently, Alice was quite partial to a panatella with George;

especially after their evening supper, when George would recurrently (and oftentimes out of the blue) verge in 'yap' overdrive. Once when Alice was in an unusually loquacious state of mind, she recounted to Sandra how on one particular occasion George wittered on for over three hours about the 'exciting' escapades of one specific hen. She also recalled that afterwards she practically felt like hara-kari would be a consolation! The reality was that she really was besotted with George. "He is the most altruistic person I have ever known".

If it was raining soup, Bob would be caught with a fork in his hand! At this juncture he was attending to supper requirements of Limberlost's only two customers this side of the 20th Century; Bob had drawn the short straw once again! In any event he looked ridiculous in his waiter's garb, unless he was serving at the "Last Supper" – he's in all probability several years older than Christ!!

It was George who spoke first – he thought that if anyone should be blamed, it should be him. Withal Kim had left him in charge of matters. He chuntered "I'm really sorrowful for the way that it's worked out Mom. I'm as hurting as you – we all are. Mom, make no mistake Lamar Smith is about as straight as a loon's leg and he's never been toilet trained in all of his godforsaken life.

The crux of the matter was our recently elected mayor: head of the town council is franchisee of the newly acquired 'Cottage Inn'

96

and as such had decided that no alcoholic beverage can be served without a specific ordinance from him. Although he has no authority to revoke Limberlost's existing liquor licence, he was, however, able to restrict its hours of trading. In a round about way it virtually was equivalent to the same – distinctly to local trade from the village

---

The out of the blue manifestation of Mom in 'physical form' was comparatively unnerving or at least a slight bit disconcerting to older members of the Cottage Inn staff who knew her by reputation. However, the Mayor – to whom she was an unknown quantity – continued on gulping down his breakfast; hunched over like a skunk eating potato bugs. His obliviousness to the little-bitty old lady descending upon him was unquestionably beyond comparison though a shade intimidating to onlookers.

Moms first impression of Mayor Lamar Smith was that he was a self-possessed hustler, who has grandiose thoughts that he is blessed with a nine-inch prick, a twelve-inch tongue and can breathe through his ears. Just presently, she was about to disprove that belief and bring him back to terra firma fast. "Yea, yea, yea" she rummaged to herself "if my aunt had nuts, she'd be my uncle!"

Looking down upon him like she was his ten foot tall mom-ma, she quipped "How come you're aiming to operate two restaurants when you don't know frog shit from pea soup!" Mayor Smith looked up from his breakfast in astonishment and shock; dribbling beads of slobber down his double chin. By now Mom had jumped aboard the bandwagon of total obnoxiousness – she never let up for an instant; "Mr, you've got a dogs attitude, if you can't eat it, you'll fuck it or piss on it; Mr, you would bugger a dragonfly if you could profit from the Vaseline – you would wouldn't you?" And just then her voice went into a high frequency "Mr, my mother has shot better men than you for $50.00 and right now I'm in a temper in search of my mother's hissy fits – so here's the deal: "You take your ordinance and put it where a monkey puts its nuts, or else I'm coming in here every morning and piss in your cornflakes; you got it?"

The puck went Mom's way. She never heard hide not hair from Anville's Mayor apart from a Christmas greeting card which carried a humorously 'bumpy' message as follows:

"Your mother should have held her waters and drowned you whilst the world had a chance!"

Kind regards Lillian

Redvers Lamar-Smith

Mom smiled mischievously, it was a knowing smile, a wily smile "Touche" she repeated "Touche" and winked resolutely at all in sundry.

That evening, watching an old Bette Davis movie in glamorous black and white – flames in the fireplace dancing menacingly in the background as Bette ascends the marble staircase. A sweet little snub-nosed revolver in Bette's hand; intending to snuff her ex-lover. The fur coat he brought her draped loosely over her slim shoulders. Mom sniffed "Oh lovely, oh lethal entanglements. In such a world could they be true? That would really be about hunky-dory with me"

I guess it's all about downright first impressions when all is said and done and a garland of chrysanthemums, for their Mom!

CHAPTER XIX
The Legacy

The gossip about Bliss & Renek was like a candy bar in the hands of pernicious children; it was not permitted to linger too long on any one pair of lips before it was passed on quickly to another.

The story goes that after Renek's abrupt departure the so-called progress of Bliss Carmen's every-increasing belly was served remorselessly along with the meat and potatoes at every supper table in Anville.

Up until Renek's departure Bliss really didn't give a burp about all the uncharitable, petty-minded scuttlebutts. Indeed, she considered it kind of 'exciting' to be having a child by ones 'foreign' lover. Whilst the parents of adolescent girls were using Bliss as an example to drive home chastity to their daughters, the daughters themselves were in awe and wonderment of Bliss & Renek: "do you suppose he's a good lover, do Polish men have huge thingamajigs?" Exciting, unanswerable, questions, tinged with jealousy and mystique...and then Renek's departure!

It's a strange world where everyone and all – Catholic, Congregationalist, Protestant and so-called Christian minded

Evangelistic mother's sons can smirk with mean self-righteousness; given the opportunity. It's almost as if they have found what they have been searching for at long last.

Sometimes, certain possessions almost become defiantly impossible to black-out from our mind or indeed to toss into the proverbial trash can. Like, for instance, the happy-go-lucky fond memories of a first love – they are our memento's of the heart. Or perhaps like keepsakes, useless mementos of a singular past but they still bring back the memories that dwell in our heart.

Of course, the well kept secret about remembering is almost entirely dependent upon trying to forget in the twinkling of an eye – or at the very least, being able to recall it on a whim, if one so desires. Or in the awfully dire event that pain is overwhelmingly dictating the odds; to well and truly bury those unproductive memories and mementos: (a) in the very hindmost isolations of the mind, or (b) in the sterile bore hole between the thriving impasto tree and the bursting cesspit.

Thank God all this happened long before constipation, indigestion, piles and morning sickness begat the obligatory instituted waddle of Bliss's pregnancy because 'burying' was precisely Bliss's solution and when the snow cleared and the ground softened, she carried it out.

There may have been a rendezvous in heaven for her and Renek but on this earth she had always been the pragmatist!

101

She had kept Renek's items in unused millinery boxes on top of her oak wardrobe. It would not be fair to say that she was happy with the idea of getting rid of them but that era was drawing to a close. She methodically wrapped each article in scraps of torn bed linen and carefully placed them in a chest where her Earle had once kept her hunting gun.

There was an essence of fundamental acceptance in her demeanour as she catalogued each object accordingly in her ledger:

1: Iver Johnson .22–calibre pistol

2: 1oz nub of gold unearthed at Bonanza Creek (Klondike)

3: Lady of the Lake – Novel by Walter Scott

4: Pack of cards with four pairs of deuces!

5: Written poetry, songs & verse

6: Military tunic

And on the top of the paraphernalia; a letter.

She locked the chest, placed an old bicycle chain around the handle and attentively lowered the obstacle down the bore hole. By the time she'd brought the shovelling to an end, you would never have known that Renek had ever drawn breath in Southern Ontario, excepting for a surviving side effect and a little fluttering movement within her.

Although Renek was gone and their mementos buried and even the need for him was gone, the trust come what may, still remained. Bliss would toil to take her chances on that trust, it was the best that she could do.

CHAPTER XX
Old Deals

She could still see him now: tall in the saddle, straightening his John B, taking the reins and disappearing into the fading sunset down the lonely trail.

Joe Burke was as individual as any man could be and along with his demise a very vital part of Lillian had also died. Yet at the same time a completely new realization had delicately tapped her on the shoulder. If by all accounts she was wanting to do justice to Joe's memory it was imperative that she continued to be the same person he knew and fell in love with – not a re-launched grieved imitation.

In many respects it was arguably the case that Joe's 'passing' had invariably taken Lillian 'beyond the pale'. That is to say her boundaries of so-called acceptable behaviour would perhaps never be entirely the same as they had been previously.

She began cutting into her steak. She had prepared it precisely the way she like it; charred on the outside, rare inside. She took another bite and chewed contentedly "you missed your calling Bob; fella your build could have been a prize fighter or a gumshoe, for sure not a Limberlost waiter eh Bob!" she joked!

She had an affection for Bob, perhaps on account of his child-like nature and, moreover, he had a right-brained approach to life in general. Besides not being caught up in those usual male attitudes of dominance and power posturing – in terms of emotional territory Bob and Mom spoke the same language. Conceivably with the same tongued perfection: they both had a likeable wish to curse out loud and talk to themselves!

It didn't take Bob long to discover that Mom's favourite nightcap was either Canadian Club and water or vodka and grapefruit juice. At this disciplined moment in time it was the latter – because of the vitamins in the juice!

"My old gumshoe Bob" she reiterated as he proceeded to freshen up her drink and pour himself a tonic water. "I would like you to visit a friend of ours at the Golden Gloves Motel. His name is Mr Jim Castellano. Please give him this note". She penned a short salutation and openly handed it to Bob. "No use talking to him Bob". She contemplated. "Jim's been as deaf as a post since before '62". Bob didn't take time out to read the note Mom had written – felt it was none of his obligation to snooping at such. However, the transcript is as follows:

Dearest,
In the hope that this finds you in the best of health, would you allow me to take breakfast with you?
Until then, may the Lord bless and protect you.

Lillian Carmen (nee Provenzano)

The note was merely a euphemism for ten words of hellfire:-

"I trust you to make over what needs making over"

CHAPTER XXI
Just Deserts

Like half-forgotten jokes, surprises can oftentimes lose their awe, when relived and retold. Unless, of course, they are a planned surprise – unaccountable yet nonetheless surprising.

Down by Winter Creek Sandra was happily playing catch-ball with George's wire terrier mutt Pinder. Dashing about among the avocado trees like a six year old innocent, pert and perky and bubbling with such enthusiasm and abandon. It was nothardly possible to imagine that she could transform into an obstreperous detached diva.

In a tract where the grass had been mown, George and Miss Alice were occupied eating cucumber sandwiches and sipping chilled Lamborghini. All the time George is relating tongue-in-cheek stories of one kind or another. Some of which he is inclined to spruce up a little, figuring they may be rather too snappy for a single lady of Alice's disposition. In any event, by and by he has her laughing – quite heartily indeed!

To be perfectly candid, George's choice of setting for a picnic was not so ideally appealing as an aperitif! For sure, it was most pleasantly cool and shaded under the large impasto tree, however, the unlucky tree was also an adjacent neighbour of the Limberlost cesspit! And, from time to time, as the breeze felt obliged, some unmentionable whiffs were to be reckoned on! Though it didn't appear to bother George an iota. He had indicated to Bob that the odious pong recounted fond memories for him – of latrine duties in WWII North Africa!

It was Wednesday afternoon and so consequently at the Humming Bird Club in downtown Toronto, Dahlia was actively enjoying herself by earning a quick buck coaching a number of Jacques' showgirls. Her choreography of exotic dance routines was seriously second to none. Apparently, several years ago she was hired as Ann Margaret's 'pinch-hitter' during Miss Margaret's rehabilitation after an accident. Now, with most tutors it's purely all down to technique, however, Dahlia's take on 'exotic' verged more upon 'erotic' – it sort of became an overindulged incestuous incarnation of her unique sexuality; understatedly it was Dahlia's definitive forte: She was a valuable asset to the studio – and they knew it. Dahlia would teach those girls more wrinkles than Methuselah's armpit. For example, she even had a trick whereby at the nipple point of her dress, she had a 10 ½ millimetre pearl sewn in to give her breasts a finished, confirmed 'pointed' look.

Dahlia knew all the ploys, prestigious and otherwise, she had even taught some of the other practitioners some of her sucker punches...only some! She was most unashamedly the quintessential pro!

Mom and Bob were sat upon canvas deckchairs under a giant palm tree, which Mom had acquired from some Middle Eastern dude whose business had gone to the dogs. Throughout the winter she had wrapped-up the tree in bubble wrap to protect it and by one means or another it had managed to survive.

Bob had a predilection to engage Mom in informative conversation; it was as though he had finally found a benefactor who approved of him. Mom would never pooh, pooh any of his observations no matter how half-baked they may seem to middle-of-the-road folk. Like on that very Wednesday afternoon when they were deliberating over Fay Wray, Manhattan and King Kong. Bob remarked that he considered Wray's relationship with Kong "unnatural" and added, "she's a tart and he's an ape!" Mom just nodded in agreement and maintained a scrupulously straight face throughout. She wasn't into the habit of undermining the worth of folk she had a fondness for.

Just another sunny Wednesday afternoon in May, a seemingly uneventful day to relax and enjoy trivial pleasures and conversation with friends – at least that's the way it was on the face of things, ostensibly so!

Redvers Lamar-Smith was the ostentatious owner of the 1957 Eldorado Brougham. It was hand-built, limited-edition Sedan and probably the most expensive car built in American at that time. The car was decadence on wheels and even had two gas tanks! It was a vehicle to die for and Lamar Smith generously obliged. It was common knowledge that he reckoned on the straight approach road to Anville as being his 'runway' but he didn't figure on a two tyre blow-out on Shanawdithit bend – it was one curve too many for Lamar-Smith! When he hit the pylon the electricity went out in Anville for several hours. The impact produced sparks, igniting one gas tank and as the car spun around the other tank exploded. The car was too hot to be touched until the following day. The Fire Chief said that all that was left of Lemar-Smith was his jewellery!

Be all that as it may, the most profound 'out of the blue' surprise that springs to mind on that sunny Wednesday afternoon was poor old George catching his 'ass' upon a rusted bicycle chain which was carelessly sticking-up out of the grass. On account of the close proximity of the cesspit, Sandra and Alice hustled the protesting 'patient' along to Brantford Medical Centre for a tetanus or anti-bacteria vaccination. It was all absolutely something of an event for George who seemed kind of 'hyper' over all the attention he was receiving; and the re-telling of his 'catastrophe'.

Meanwhile Mom and Bob were carefully examining it...the mysterious rusty chain – not George's ass! After some spade work they discovered that it was attached to an ancient gun chest.

Mom asserted how peculiar it all was, that such inexplicable goings-on could occasion themselves on an ordinary sunny Wednesday afternoon. "Whatever will unearth itself next Bob?" Her question and frowning frown, they indicated that she was trying to second-guess!

CHAPTER XXII
Endings & Beginnings

When know-it-all's are given to claim that nothing significant goes on in so-called humdrum municipalities such as Anville, at what half-cocked point would they be inclined to defer their judgement? To some extent it may be argued that pretty much all comparatively 'discreditable' occurrences do hastily become community 'property' with such uncontrollable enthusiasm and vigour that by the time all the muck is well and truly raked, there is hardly any enjoyment by replication: Like ice-cubes in booze, the ferocity is lessened! However, every so often there are a mixed variety of small town shames that for the time being are altogether quite unmentionable. These maligned snippets are customarily buried just minusculy below the surface, ready to rear up in the event of necessity at a future date.

If God had wished to smile upon those for whom He otherwise had very little time for, then perchance the discovery of Bliss Carmen's gun chest was a sign of great divine favour.

"Like the treasure chest off the old Hispaniola" Bob declared quite elaborately. "I dunno Bob" Mom retorted doubtfully. It was as though she was fearful of what hellacious hello's and sallow salutations it may contain. She knew that Bliss's love was similar in nature to an enigmatic silver bell tied carefully about the throat of a wraith-like cat – sometimes sounding near and reposed and at other times sounding far away and reproachful.

Mom gave Bob an unenthusiastic half smile – there was a negligible plea in the tone of her words "save me from the terrible pterodactyl please Bob". There was something about the amount of black hair on his hugely primal hands that caused her to say it!

November 11th 1918

The weather was beginning to break-up on that bitter anxiety ridden burying day – this was to be Bliss Carmen's especial 'fait accompli' although she didn't yet know it per-se.

Bliss had awakened from her dreams with an unusual start; she had dreamt how she meticulously tore-up and burned the only photograph of her lover and smeared all the shrapnel pieces upon her face and body. It was not a good start to the day!

Bliss wasn't a particularly religious person; church going and such, but she did put a lot of trusting in the Good Book. As a child her Cree nanny had taught her the words: "I was lost and undone but I am saved by the blood of the Crucified One". In those bygone days she never really understood the implication of their meaning or, for that matter, their importance but before the day was through she would bathe in those words; she would cradle them in her every deliberation.

Perhaps part of the enduring fallaciousness of the Good Book is that it contains such an exciting and a formidable assortment of almost sentient skeletons. If all their bony remains were pieced together it would create an anatomy of scandalous falsehoods to rival even Alice in Wonderland! On the other hand perhaps the Good Book is both exact and exacting because on that fateful burying day there really was a considerable amount of heavenly involvement around.

In any event it was most certainly a special day of phenomenal occurrences. What went down on November 11th was more than suggestive of so-called 'heavenly involvement'. Before evening dusk had settled, Germany was signing an armistice; Babe Ruth's pitching helped Boston Red Sox beat Chicago Clubs; and Jim Buck President of Anville's Royal Bank was apprehended crossing Rainbow Bridge with $75,000!

Now, if all else is unbelievable regarding the aforementioned heavenly involvement then most surely some credibility should be given to ex-president Mr Jim Buck who most emphatically protested 'his' blamelessness by declaring (quote) "it wasn't greed that motivated me; it was purely because the Lord gave me a curious desire to find out if I could get away with it!"

So, back to whether or not anything or nothing much goes on in so-called uninteresting municipalities such as Anville; perhaps then it really all depends upon a person's demographic point of view!

For example, it's true that the chests of city folk are frequently in the most shameful disarray. However, exaggerated tittle-tattle is generally tossed out with next day's coffee grains; there is always an abundant quantity available in the city. Contrary to the small town whispers which have a more than uncanny knack of perseverance and longevity. It's all down to the effect of intimacy that breeds in smaller communities – that's the main difference and nothing more besides.

However, when all is said and done, whether city or small town, there are only four types of 'discreditable' occurrences which are odds-on to make excellent blether-blather: robbery, murder, suicide and last but not least, the impregnation of an unmarried woman. The latter being by far the most serious discreditable occurrence of them all.

After Renek left her – during the night, after Bliss had acquainted him that she was having his child; she went at once to her Godfather - the head of the family.

He was a gentleman in any familiar sense of the word and a person of staunch family loyalties – his values overrode everything else. Although he was both rich and immensely powerful, it was somewhat amusing that he rarely wore anything more elaborate than baggy khaki trousers and a grimy shirt. Visitors quite often would mistake him for the gardener. He surely didn't get to be head honcho by any subtlety and Reneks conduct did not sit well with him at all. Stony-faced he left Bliss under no illusion about his "contempt for the sin of bastardcy" and something about "an incinerator for his (Renek's) wickedness".

Bliss was slightly shocked and disturbed by the literal connotation of some of her Godfather's words and so when after several months they had failed to find Renek, she was to some extent quite relieved.

They had opened doors in every sweatshop, hauliers, croppers and even stevedores in the docks. The word had well and truly gone out and every employer who hired scab labour responded throughout Ontario; but Renek seemed to have melted away for good.

Bliss sat cross-legged in her favourite rocking chair for a long time, unwaveringly waiting for something to happen; but nothing did happen. Her lips remained unmoved and tightly compressed; it was almost as though she was not breathing...because Renek still breathed and breathed his way right through her!!

CHAPTER XXIII
Synapse

The opening of the chest –

Lillian didn't know what her thoughts and secret wishes were but she knew she'd earned the right to ignore the breakfast foray today – time for the staff to get to grips!

She was trying to appear (to herself and others!) entirely composed, thinking of other things rather than the emotional deliberation of opening the chest; moreover the contents contained within!

Her thoughts were travelling like wild fire through a denial check list: "I'll go through to Inn on the Twenty this coming weekend...or maybe take a train to Augerge Du Vieux-Port and then likely look in on Kim and Jacques" (Lillian did enjoy the sight of the green fields and poppies from the train observation car). Her whole thought process had become well and truly muddled; it was similar in nature to trying to make up your bed whilst you are still in it! At the final point in her muddled checklist she began scouting through her address book of long-forgotten names: "Perhaps I'll visit superstitious old England – stop over in Somerset; always liked that name for some reason".

By the late afternoon she had become almost as sick of prevaricating as she was with confronting the issue and as the day began to draw to a close it was only her inborn cussedness that brought her to the end of her tether.

Ever since the disconcerting discovery of the proverbial chest it was as though God Himself had been playing a game of bridge with her and now finally he was wearisome and wished to dissolve the partnership and show her his hand. In any event, the whole hullabaloo was altogether relative because when the chips were down Lillian would rather have pins in her eyes than to become a witless scaredy-cat...in the first instance how could she really be that certain that the chest was Bliss's and for that matter that it was directed to her: Oh she 'knew'; she unwillingly 'knew'!

Alone at last and now finally forever, for good, once and for all, the moment of truth: there were no mirrors to see herself in, just Lillian and Bliss – her beloved adversary! Lillian's attention was down to one line only: to open 'that' chest and to come to terms with the consequences – there would definitely 'be' consequences, there always were with Bliss! However, overriding the prophets of doom there was perhaps a positive side to the equation; Bliss herself had taught her that sometimes change is a good commodity to acquaint yourself with. Like the seasons (sometimes harsh) but quite often just by their nature, something positive is learned from them. For all one knows this April evening may be the turning fork for the future, who knows?

Bliss had left the brass key in its lock, seemingly for convenience purposes or perhaps not knowing what to do with it otherwise!

118

Lillian soberly lifted the lid – if anything had jumped out she could have killed it by the 'draconian' expression on her face!

On the top of various appurtenances of doom lay this pretty little-bitty literary work of Walter Scott which inscribed in gold leaf read 'Lady of the Lake'. The hard cover contained a photogravure of an Edwardian lady holding a faded blue parasol. Peeping somewhat faint-heartedly from the slightly yellowish pages, a sturdy umber envelope (the type used to send important military dispatches) and written in bold black ink across the entire length of the envelope the inimitable words: 'INTENDED FOR THE EYES OF LILLIAN CARMEN ONLY'. The intensity of the writing (accentuated by deep underlining) to some extent gave the impression of being threatening to interlopers – no doubt that was the objective!

CHAPTER XXIV

The Confession

Mon Cheri,

I gaze at you lie sleeping by the side of me and wonder whether this message will ever find you. Perhaps it is enough that I have written it and perhaps you should be allowed to sleep whilst I attempt to close the gaps in time and space for self-absorbed me. I know that as you grow older our connection will become telepathised – as it did between my mother and me – and for that reason you will in all likelihood perceive the truth even though it may not be visible.

When approaching the turn of the Century Earle gave me a rifle for my thirtieth birthday, the vow for such an impressive gift (and I readily agreed to it) was that I would shoot my first deer, for him, for our winter stockpile – this was normally a task reserved exclusively for Earle. He was able to teach me some real fancy shooting, before the pneumonia got him and he met his maker in November 1901. Then, like the Holy Ghost was tallying his accounts, your sister Lillian also became afflicted with a similar debility and passed away the following February. Doc Maclaine said it was an unfortunate case of phthisis disease or it could have been a strain of pneumonia but he couldn't be sure. It would be impossible for me to attempt to articulate my emptiness and in any event that kind of loss is too inhuman to confer; enough to say that I never want to meet it face to face again.

Last year a traveller stopped-off at Limberlost, a Polish exile. His name was Renek Comanescu – he was your father Lillian!!

Men are usually men but even the worst and most vulgar of them are appreciative comfort for a few seconds in the dark. Renek was neither worst nor vulgar but neither was he on any account my husband. From the onset our special relationship was completely without contract or condition. I knew in my heart that Renek was always just a passer-by and passers-by do what passers-by do; they just pass by! I was out to capture as much warmth and tenderness that I could; and missed during the barreness of many years alone. I guess that along the line somewhere the line began to grow shorter and my skin shadowed, and his need grew weaker, until finally, expectably and unexpectedly I woke up and he had gone! It was both as simple and intense as that: no more, no less.

Although there was no misery in not being loved any longer, there was in not loving; be that as it may he had left me with love in abundance, my tattoo of ownership; you my handsome Lillian.

It wasn't long before my conscience ridden guilt succeeded in wrecking my rose coloured perspectives and I began the adulterous journey of self-worthlessness; it was as though my selfishness had tarnished my vows to Earle.

In total bewilderment, one restless night, I removed Earle's gift from the gun chest and in defiance of my vows I threw it hard as

121

I could into Winter Creek. This empty gun chest contains the remainder of the vows I broke during my involvement with Renek.

As you grew into womanhood I lacked the capability to divulge my shamefulness to you and instead I deceived you into believing that your father was Earle and had died during 1917 and that you had a namesake who also died so prematurely at the same time. Please find me in your heart and forgive me Lillian. You and I will always be connected; we are a synapse in the whole of eternity – of this I am positive.

As one
Mother

The afternoon shadows were gathering as Lillian's day began to go home. It was that strange light of the in-between time when you long for the daylight to stay but the darkness is insistent.

Alone, she repeated her mother's name, softly at first and then slightly louder to be sure she could be heard.

There was an ethereal quality to the sign of the wind and the rustling from the trees as though they were speaking back to her.

Lillian reflected that it was rightful that they would always be connected: Like the venerable ivy that clings so fervently to the Limberlost, Bliss still clings, even though she no longer remains.

CHAPTER XXV

..."and the hunter, home from the hill"

Robert Louis Stevensons Requiem

Occasionally in life, at a certain yet unpredictable moment in time, you may reach a kind of impasse situation. You may question it and it will slowly become clear to you that in this instance there aren't anywhere near enough stars in the heavens to console yourself with. The usually faithful majority have all but given-up or disappeared straight away and the remainder have, for unknown reasons, simply become indifferent.

For all that, when you walk the streets of invisibility; and nightly without hesitation those so-called inanimate mannequins cat-call you from their department store windows, is it blatantly so obvious? Conceivably they shriek and stare at your uncertainty because the answer to your question is so marvellously within your heart, yet occasionally you are unable to locate it by yourself.

Then, by coincidence you awaken; without warning the telephone is ringing, there's an unequivocal answer and your new kindred soul arrives on the block...

The locomotive slowed; its carriages glancing past shanties and shabby dilapidated buildings before it pulled into Anville with a long scouring stop. She stepped jovially off the train and paused purposefully, looking around thoroughly, nothing had changed - not one speck. Exactly the same as she had remembered it: the raggedy wooden waiting room, the severely pitched roof and the Gothic style windows that gave it the air of a broken-down church. Nailed haphazardly to the North side of the building was a well weathered sign which read; ANVILLE – POP. 937. She hesitated and grinned, "nine hundred and thirty seven – sounds like the price of a new suit to me!"

No other passengers debarked from the train which was surprising because at six thirty in the evening you would have expected someone to have been commuting. For all the lack of activity going on, it might just have been midnight. She wondered how long it would take – how many more 'Our Fathers' and 'Hail Mary's' would be required to keep development at bay; another fruitless century perhaps? She stopped to watch the train slowly disappearing down the curving railroad tracks and smiled a knowing smile at the long drawn-out wail as it crossed the steel bridge over Winter Creek. She was stronger now from all the happenstance that had happened and that will not go on happening; a rekindled glow of excitement was leaping in her heart; likely because she was so kindredly close to home.

Limberlost was just hanging loose and chilling out – generally taking a well earned respite ahead of the evening onslaught!

It was that anonymous between time of late afternoon and early evening when more often than not the sociable class are 'resuscitating' themselves. That is to say they are in the process of showering the day's debris away and bonnieing themselves for their evening excursions. As a general rule this 'brashness' to water did not appeal itself to Bob ever since he became acquainted with 'Grocer's Itch'. Now this was a kind of inflammatory skin disease which was caused by handling sugar and flour. Mom had told him to keep his bowels well open and not to wash with soap (and no scratching!), However, it was her Tar Lotion treatment that finally purged the disease. From that point on, Bob's ablutions took only a weekly observance!

Right now Bob wanted to savour his soup: it was rich and thick – tomatoey with just the right touch of garlic. Recently, Mom had suggested (with a great deal of subtlety) that Bob should consider wearing a 'smart' necktie whilst attending his restaurant duties. "It would be inclined to give you the air of authority deserved of you Bob – put you apart from the girls". It wasn't as though there was anything resembling a 'dress code' for either staff or customers; Mom simply required Bob to 'button-up' the graphic pictorials upon his brawny chest and this seemed to her the subtlest way to wangle it!

She had especially washed, ironed and starched a nice personable blue stripped tie which she acquired from her mother's odds and end. When she finally presented it to Bob he looked as thrilled as a dog being let out for a wee. She several times guided him through the loop and knot procedure and in all fairness, it looked pretty good on him when eventually it took pride of place around his 20" neck.

Mom was always a sucker for detail but it had to be good, couldn't be bad and certainly not indifferent – and she found 'gaudy' intolerable. Which brings to mind that just of late Dahlia's ultra short frocks were receiving attention; particularly from the trucking fraternity who had taken to smoking 'Winston' cigarettes located on the top shelve: but that's another story entirely!

In any event, although he was much to pussy to say so, bashful Bob was becoming plentifully pissed off with 'that' girl Dahlia and with Sandra also for that matter. It transpired that from time to time the old crank brain was allowing himself to be 'bought off' with rich Havana cigars in consideration of taking over the girls shifts. Said that the only thing he'd been able to liberate at the Bay of Pigs Little Snafu was several boxes of Swisher & Son Havana's and the uncontrollable urge for same. Similar to his buddy George, Bob too had fond memories of distinctive aroma's from his past but unlike George's memories Bobs were somewhat more sophisticated in nature!

The girls had found Bob's Achilles heel and he knew it. He sneered to himself "bet they are off alley-cattin at that Bamboo Club again". On occasion it genuinely appeared that Bob was thoroughly aggravated when in fact he was quietly in very good spirits. It was a type of contented variation that in its own way soothed him down. George, who knew Bob better than most,

126

referred to Bob's incongruity as a "merciful fortunality"; which when explained meant that it was Bob's unique psychological safety valve that prevented Bob from killing someone!

So, there it is and taking into account all of Bob's daily blessings, his pseudo annoyance face, his payola Havana's and his most stupendous tomatoey soup; this evening he appeared to be in his seventh heaven...unless a customer should stray unwisely and unwittingly through the entrance door!

There was a melancholic cloud hanging uncomfortably over Limberlost ever since Mom had unearthed her box of tricks. Overall, you could cut the atmosphere with a knife and without exception the feelings were affecting the whole caboodle of things: every person, creature, nook, cranny and floorboard throughout the entire edifice were empathizing with Mom's heartbreak.

George and Alice especially were perhaps more-so consternatious because singularly it had been them (or George's derrière!) that had unearthed the whole nasty can or worms in the first place.

George was so concerned about Mom that it would incense him with anger; Alice was more caught up in the utter exasperation of the whole shenanigans and the possibility of it effecting George's health.

George and Alice sat contemplating, watching the two grass sprinklers making lazy circles. George wiped a solitary tear from his eye "you hardly ever can being back old times" he paused and then continued "Mom should have kept those old ghosts in the chest and just burned the godforsaken thing!" Alice nodded in agreement several times over; like all that nodding would somehow alleviate the precariousness of George's emotions. However, George was beginning to be wrathful once again, "when I was a P.O.W. in North Africa I once placed a rescue note in a bottle and carefully threw it into the ocean. It's almost probably still bobbing around out there somewhere, waiting to be found" Alice smiled at him understandingly. George pressed on "the point is Alice; there is no advantage in it ever being found 'cause there aint anyone out there to rescue anymore!"

The way that George felt inclined was, that Mom had paid all of her tabs in full; and that being the case she was more than entitled to some peace of mind and an occasional break from looking after all and sundry. She didn't need anything plush or of an exaggerated nature, just some recognition once in a while, so that one day she doesn't recognize that the sad old lady in the mirror is really her!

George quietly and calmly looked through his grey bushy eyebrows at his Alice's handsomely lovely face and reflected, "sometimes folk think that it's easier to leave than to be left behind; I don't ever want Mom to either leave or to fancifully imagine that she's been left behind !"

Lillian was trying her utmost to navigate between a crippling error and a brutal truth; bizarre circumstances to be straight-off plunged into by any stretch of the imagination.

Foremostly, the elusive answer she desired of what exactly was going down here was the question to the question mark between her instinct and her rationality. It was kind of like posting a letter but not knowing the postal address. Was she cheated? She felt cheated! Was she deceived? She felt deceived! Yet surely the years justify all those folded up and hidden things. The insouciance of giving the game away to a death sister and walking away – hello Lillian, good-bye Lillian, a namesake; no more, no less. And embracing the incredibility of responding to a life sister. Where would she go from there?

Lillian's revelations – as told to 'Pinder Zalokostas:_

There couldn't have been a finer portion of space set aside for contemplative purposes than among the shaded evergreens on the grassy banks of Winter Creek. And there could not have been a finer placebo than Pinder the mutt to be contemplative with. Why even a so-called shameful sin can become somewhat less toxic to its holder once the narration of same has been shared; even if the supposed listener has not the slightest comprehensible idea of what on earth is being recounted! Many a despondent soul have found an answer to the question that

129

they were afraid to ask, among the shaded evergreens on the grassy banks of Winter Creek.

When time has whirled and twirled and well-nigh danced itself into oblivion, certain memories of a sympathetic or sentimental nature can become out of focus, out of frame. They have this curious inclination to become either overemphasised or even less conspicuous than they had in actuality been; miscible sketches and modified contradictions of the truth.

Then there are the other type of memories, the acidic type, the type that can only be recollected with tight fists and yet somehow have the resilient tenacity to survive perfectly as clear and precise today as they were yesterday and indeed will be tomorrow.

For as good as not it is almost effortless when calling to mind the way in which Limberlost has evolved and how it has transformed itself and the lives of all the souls who have lived and loved here over the years.

When recalling the way it was to the way it is, I guess like all of us it has matured somewhat; and yet there is something about its maturity that has a freshness about it.

I still recall the winter of 1923. Mother said that it was the 'most perishing' winter since '99 that she could think back on; and I have no doubts that it was. The thermometer on the back porch lintel was reading minus 35 degrees and had barely deviated for weeks.

Mother and me had resorted to utilising the food storeroom as our make-shift abode. It was likely the only habitable room in the building – Mother said it was because of the cavity walls. There was only one small window to worry about, even so our breath was condensating to ice on the inside of the window glass so we couldn't really see out, excepting for whether it was day or night time. Leastways, for the time being, we had an abundance of good dry firewood – which was perhaps the most unthreatening feature of those times. Earle had downed trees and created the plot for Limberlost years previous. The residual lumber had been lying under a tarpaulin year in year out since Earle's demise.

Mother and me were disinclined to interfere with that tarpaulin for fear we may butt in on an unspecified amount of snakes or rats! That weren't going to worry us under the present circumstances because them there rodents would be frozen solid for sure.

Although it didn't seem to make a whole lot of difference how plentiful we built the fire up; the cloths we wore would become so hot we were unable to touch them and yet our bodies were still cold, incredulously, painfully, bitter cold.

That lousy winter appeared to alter Mother, it made her become almost unrecognizable at times. It was as though all of her customary optimistic fevour had somehow in itself reached its own freezing point and kind of been decimated beyond reckoning.

I recall her bellyaching an awful lot over how she really hated this country. "Iniquitous Siberian Canada" she referred to it as. Every each time it would follow with "I wish we was home in Virginia".

Yes, during that brief interim period of out and out self-realization, Mother revealed herself as the typical curmudgeon; although I guess that it endeared her to me even more than I could have imagined: perhaps because, for once, she had shown the normally resistant chink in her emotional armour.

There were oceans of stuff that went down during that abysmal winter of 1923. It's surprising how all these years later it's only the insignificant goings-on that tend to replay themselves in my memory. For example, I never could accustom myself to the round-the-clock howls of the wolves. In the beginning it used to unnerve me some until Mother clued me in. She said that the poor creatures were not simply howling, "they were crying and lamenting their grief". "Can you imagine how cold and desperately hungry they must be Lillian". In the time following late February we neither heard or saw hide nor hair of them. Mother said they'd more than likely moved-on but I always had a horrible belief that perhaps they'd died all alone out there in the forest.

_____

Throughout the long awaited Summer of '23 Harry Garofolo's maintenance vehicle had almost become a permanent fixture, parked-up outside the Limberlost. Mother's determination to make restitutions for our winter sufferings was well and truly reflected in her new avant-garde Limberlost – why we even had a telephone connection and a women's rest room installed.

The complications during that unpleasant winter had been exacerbated because, apparently, Earle had not at all bothered to stud some of the principal structural walls. I recall several bedtimes when it seemed uncertain that we would pull through the night. Mother and me would gather together and she would say a prayer for us. Sometimes I would drawing-pin a note addressed to Jesus to the outside lintel – it had always disappeared by the coming morning. I guess all we ever thought about was the weather and whether we could endure another night's battering.

Strange though it may seem now, from time to time Mother would suggest that I should do some genuflexions to the winter sun. Said that in awful event we freeze in our sleep, each genuflexion I made would be recorded on my death certificate to God – as a kind of resume to my respectfulness of Him!

I truly believe that our chances of survival were pretty low, especially after our antiquated generator kept short circuiting and leaving us in unthinkable darkness. At times like those I would become so panicky scared and begin to be over talkatively loud. Mother would quickly remind me that it was more gainful to our situation to talk in short whispers – said loud and silly talk was totally unproductive and would only exaggerate our predicament by stirring-up molecules in the air and thereby use more heat!

Yes, it was true that Mother had many strange notions; perhaps they were an apropos of nothing but nonetheless, her views with regard to the nature and origins of existence and interaction of the mind could at times be quite fascinating. Shortly after Bliss' death I visited her elderly first cousin in Virginia. She told me that many of Bliss' theories had their foundations in her interest of metaphysics as a young woman.

There comes a time when fiction can overlap fact and I have no idea as to whether some of Bliss's habits had anything whatsoever to do with her beliefs. All I can do is to tell it the way I remember it; but one thing is for certain, Mother's notions were the most pure and uncontaminated explanations as she saw it; she wasn't really that bothered about who the hell Aristotle was – George the chicken farmer could have quite discourteously masqueraded as Aristotle for all she cared!

Be all as it may, not so many of my childhood recollections were of such a melancholy nature as I am leading you to believe; either during that most raw winter or any other winter for that matter.

Equally I recall the ever-so affectionate and important times that we spent together; the requite moments of unsurpassed enjoyment.

Like, for instance, every early am whilst performing our necessary ablutions. An unceremonious chore normally, but for me and Mother, bathing in cold water easily become a 'fun-run'.

We would make an immense merriment out of finding and catching all those little particles of frozen ice that were hiding in the shivering metallic basin. Mother would refer to them as being 'dead butterflies'. "Find all those dead butterflies sailing in our bath water again Lillian" she would say in a caustically fortissimo voice.

One monotonously bitter day was followed by another exactly alike. Then, as if by chance, eventually all at once it happened – just at the pivotal point when we were beginning to accept a complete indifference to our mortality. Almost overnight as though this was the awakening from a macabre fairy-story; the sky was as exquisitely blue as a '58 Pontiac Bonneville and Mr Sun was beaming at us from all sides of everywhere.

In our space enclosed by walls, floor and ceiling where we had lived like amputated remnants of civilization, thinking only about the tireless weather; without further ado the weather had decided to think about us.

That divine blush of spring had gotten started with painting its delicate icons wide, near and far. Our pensive lives were transformed and interlaced with peace of mind and planting new crops in softened earth and at the end of the day washing my hair in spring rain.

Lillian laughed out-loud "Mother we can always be together but like the banks of Winter Creek we need to be apart if the river is to remain a whole" with a solemnly civiliant tone she added "thank you Mother for making me who I am"

Before she could 'stupefy' poor Pinder with another nostalgerized dreamscape a melodious voice chimed-in on her reclusive preoccupation:

"Really good to see you again Mom"

"Kim, my darling" she cried joyfully "you caught an early train"

They threw their arms around one another, their faces glowing with impassionment, their hearts hummed and honed by perfect pitch to perfect pitch.

"So our errant father was *also* a singer" Kim chuckled cheerfully

Lillian was still clinging to her sister into the realm of one and not letting go "and a poet" she replied with much emphasis.

Sandra had been observing them both with a grinning curiosity, from a high stool in the adjacent cookhouse; whilst anticipating the finger-licking cheesecake on the plate in front of her.

She perked – "conceivably, you's father can now finally lie-down in peace". She paused, cut the cheesecake with her fork, let out a huge sigh and reiterated (slightly sarky) "conceivably!"

____ The End ____

Addendum

Can any story ever eventually be completely told – and for that matter can any story ever eventually be absolutely finished in its entirety for always and for all time? Are the subtle inferences of the author's somewhat 'prim' sentences the only necessary yardstick of conclusion, or are such as these merely soggy 'pacifiers', which we find insincere and to some extent disturbingly offensive? Conceivably, one way or another it should be our worldly-wise awareness that easily answers these questions; but is it?

Surely it must be true that if it is the case that we are only able to 'perceive' a story to be entire because of the dictatorial coaxing of its authors pen, then perhaps this pseudo formulaic dexterity has (unwittingly or otherwise) produced (and achieved) an enormous unnecessary trade-off. And in that event, the actuality of the genuine story is utterly missed or disfigured (or both) on this occasion and forevermore.

Be all that as it may, sometimes the definitive story cannot be completely told or absolutely finished for always and for all time – regardless of the author's adeptness and commitment. However, it is possible for its 'outstretched' narrative to simply be allowed to interimise – to be 'put on ice' for a while. Similarly (and without prejudice) the story could even be temporarily abandoned; leastways, if only to the extent where its fate is still quite conspicuously visible – and, therefore, semi-secure.

Although any story's future prospect may always have a kind of risky and vulnerable flavour about them, it is perhaps the story's inherent meaningfulness and honesty that sometimes dictates its longevity. In any event once the tourniquet is finally removed, the choosing of the story's destiny will undoubtedly be with the reader – the author, by their own rectitude must negate their right to opinionise or to decide.

LIMBERLOST III

(last in a trilogy)

~ available during 2015/16 ~

A Note About The Author

Ricky Dale was born in England and raised in West Africa and North America; his mother referred to the family as being of 'Colonial' nationality.

Ricky's singing career began in 1959 with one-nighters, college dates, and the occasional radio show.

As fame increased, he began to- and fro-ing across the Atlantic; giving pleasure to capacity audiences in clubs and theatres.

An individual style and heartfelt rendering of ballads, and the contrast of his wild Rock 'n Roll were, he says, 'Inspired from the hope and energy of West Africa.'

As the 60s developed Ricky began to shun the glare of celebrity. Studios, clubs, and stages pulsed with drugs; and a tragic mass entertainment of messed-up, so-called music was becoming mainstream. After a long absence from the stage, he completed contractual obligations in Niagara and Southampton, England and literally faded into obscurity.

In 2000 Ricky, with his daughter Kim, visited Canada. 'It was a kind of odyssey to the past,' he says.

Their poignant journey encompassed the Brant Inn location in Burlington, Ontario.

Decades before, as an enterprising teenager from England, he stepped into the limelight of this fabulous nightclub and truly perfected his craft.

In that golden era a host of glamorous stars entertained the Brant's sophisticated audiences. Ricky had fronted the Guy Lombardo Band, duetted with the sheer genius Danny Kaye, and had been 'mothered' by the beautiful Jayne Mansfield: 'When the old-timers were mean to me, she provided sympathetic company where I could escape at will and complain.'

'The Brant Inn was tragically torn down in around 1970; but as Kim and I stood on the shore of Lake Ontario (near Maple Avenue), we could easily imagine the melodies that had floated out across the lake: sometimes reality is not permitted to be an intruder!'

Ricky was MD of several innovative companies in the West of England for 21 years.

Lightning Source UK Ltd.
Milton Keynes UK
UKOW07f2139280115

245312UK00001B/4/P